TOFU INK ARTS PRESS

VOLUME 5

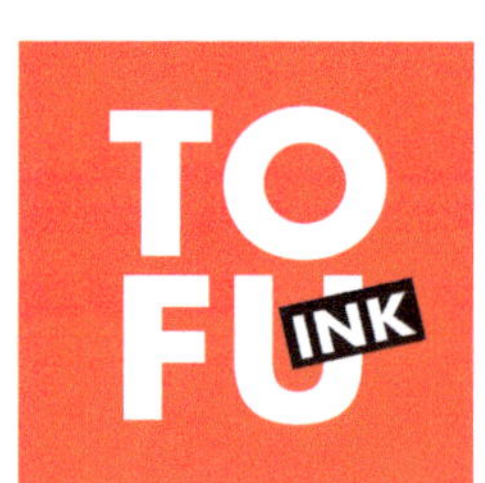

Tofu Ink Arts Press Volume 5
Copyright © 2023 by Brian L. Jacobs, Pasadena, California, USA.
Published by Tofu Ink Arts Press. All rights reserved.
Book design by JLTY Atelier
Cover image: Untitled, Oil on Canvas, 2021 by Melinda R. Smith

ISBN: 978-1-958661-05-5

www.TOFUINK.com
A member of CLMP

Dedicated to

Julie Patton, Anne Waldman, Allen Ginsberg, Elise Blankley,
Kathrine McMahon, Michael Ngo &
The Nipponzan Myohoji
who all had the most influence on my human agent

"To consecrate the union between elsewhere and possibility,
the poet demanded of himself permanent abstinence
from something impossible."

- Poetics of Relation, Edouard Glissant

CONTENTS

PREFACE

"Poetic thought creates the opportunity for an infinite sort of conjunction, perpetuated through conquests of ideas; a fantasy; it is fragile and inescapable, obscure and revealing. The future will be transcended; poetry invents its tongues."

- Poetics of Relation, Edouard Glissant

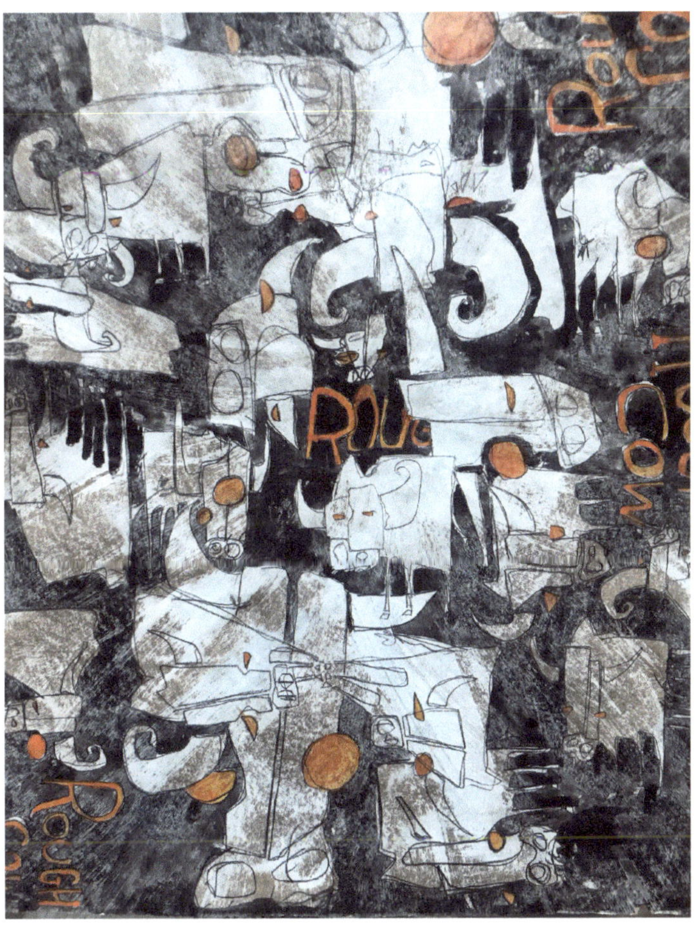

Brad O'Sullivan **Rough Cow: Collective Noun VII**

Tofu Ink Arts Press absorbs in possibilities; the possibilities our poets and artists share with our readers in our Volume 5 edition. The reader IS the writer, and we invite you to imagine! Our writers and artists rupture, mapping at times a-linearly & all proliferating, without boundaries or centers, in the margins without limits, rejecting principles of hegemony, creating a desire, that is always in flux, along new pathways of experimentation. Tofu Ink contributors manifest possibility; a sort of, what I like to call a Rhizomatic Poetic. This poetic inquiry explores diverse artistic acts; poetic discursive narratives, mutating through exploring memory, decolonizing, otherness, romanticization of the other and subsequently sometimes with elicit performances of queer identity, with overlapping Rhizomatic voices in errantry. These artists are the true auditors of our world, for discovering every possible elsewhere; a liberating vehicle into possibilities. The arts may be the only medium to weave these difficult tasks.

Tofu Ink Arts Press has come a long way in the last two years since we have been birthed. Our first issue in Spring 2021 was strictly digital moving into a format for our Summer 2021 issue as an actual journal that we eventually created as an E Reader. Our first print issue was for the beginning of 2022 and exhibited stunning pieces that we were able to exhibit at the March, 2022 AWP conference in Philadelphia, Pennsylvania with a tremendously positive response. Volume 4 shined with talent as we brought our artists internationally, for we have changed our printers, making our books available online and in every book retailer in the world.

Tofu Ink Arts Press is now venturing into new possibilities by printing single author and artist books for release this year. We are hard at work! We have twelve books we are currently working on that will be sold online and in books stores worldwide. We will also see you in Seattle for AWP 2023, with a reading panel and booth at the book fair. We are also excited about announcing in November 2022 our Poetry Prize in honor of Theatre Visionary Reza Abdoh and our new Arts, plus Chapbook contests.

Thank you Jojo for his selfless efforts in editing and digital magic. Without you we are nothing!

Please enjoy this 2023 Winter's selection of Tofu Ink Arts Press Volume 5.

Jan 2023

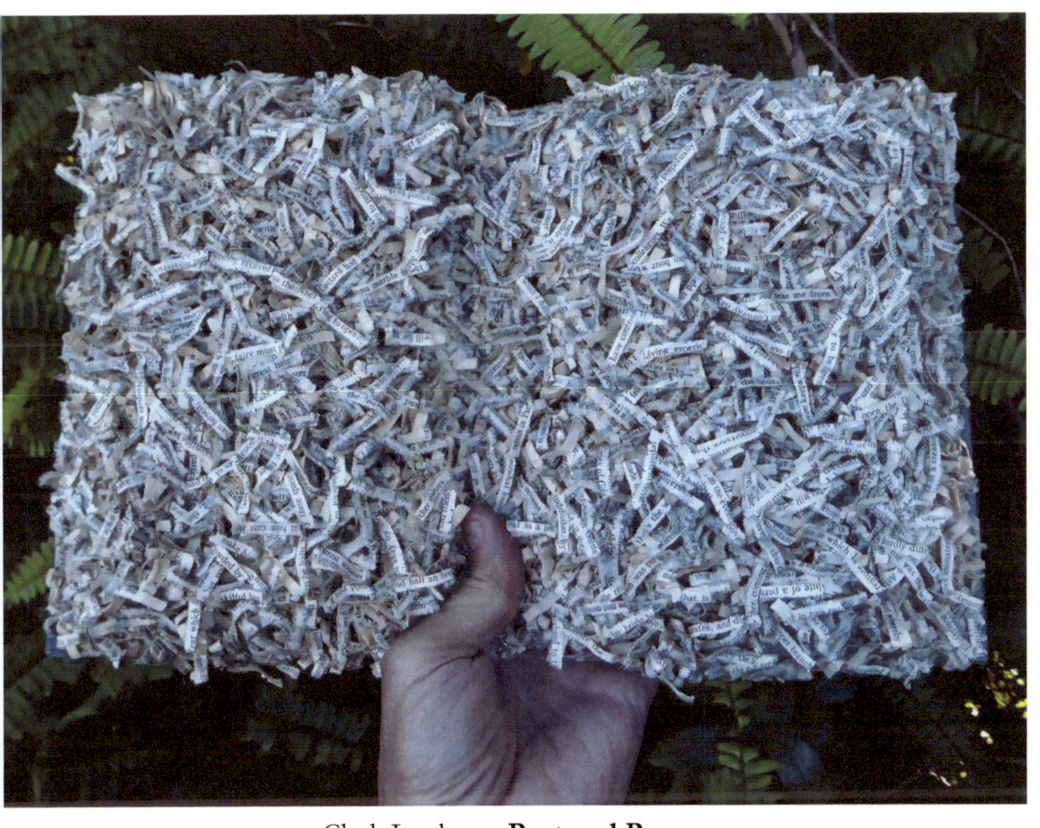

Clark Lunberry **Postcard Poems**

Featuring my deceased father's large collection of postcards,
with found fragments of language located in a shredded copy of
Marcel Proust's *Remembrance of Things Past*

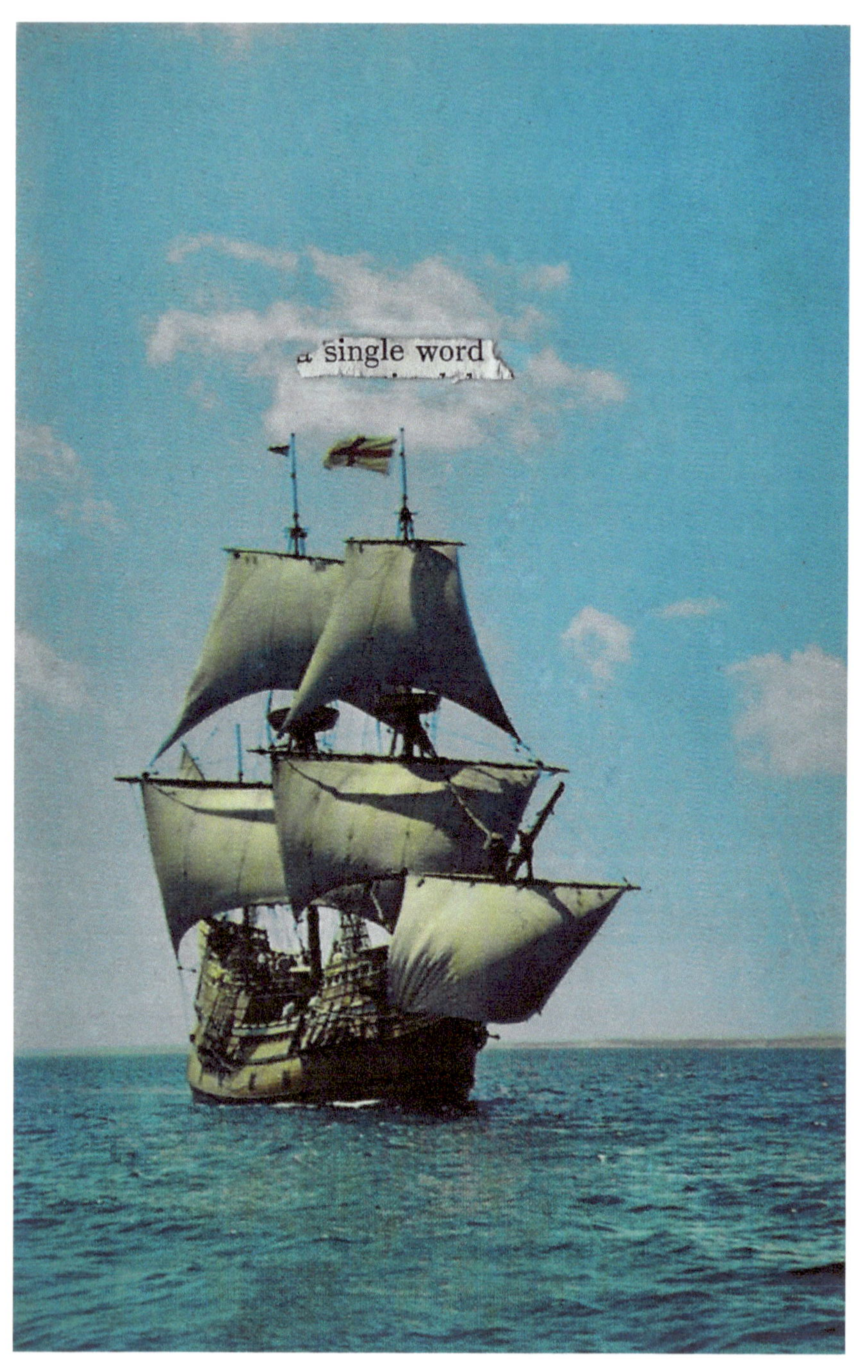

Clark Lunberry **Postcard Poems**

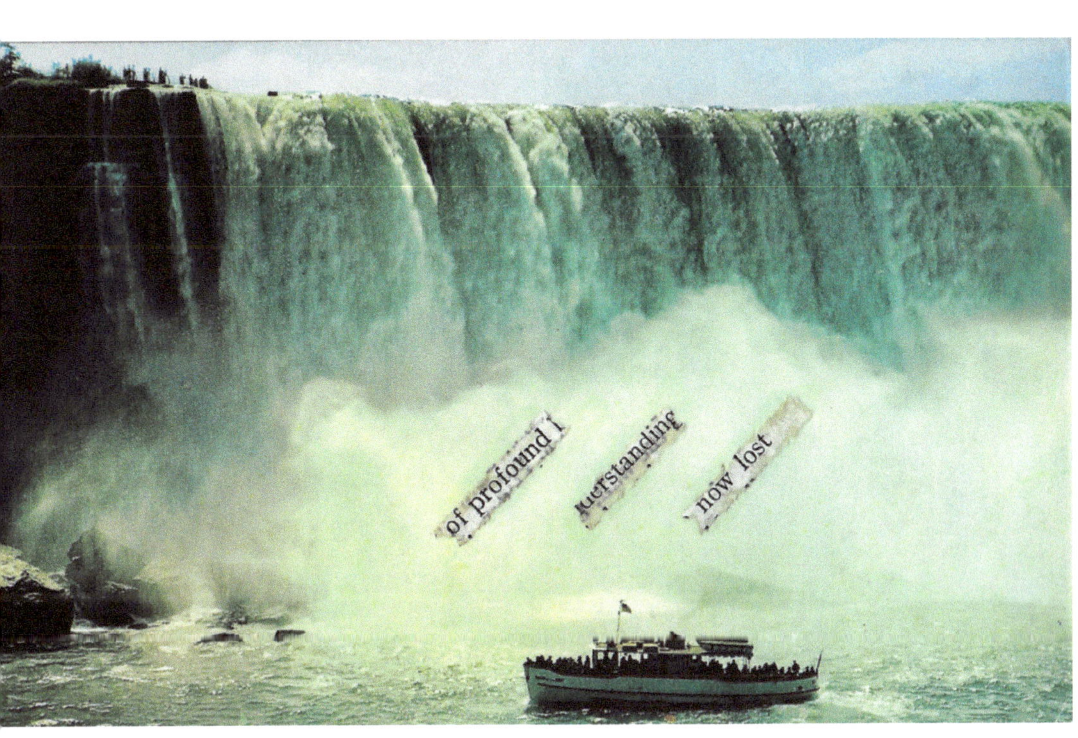

Clark Lunberry **Postcard Poems**

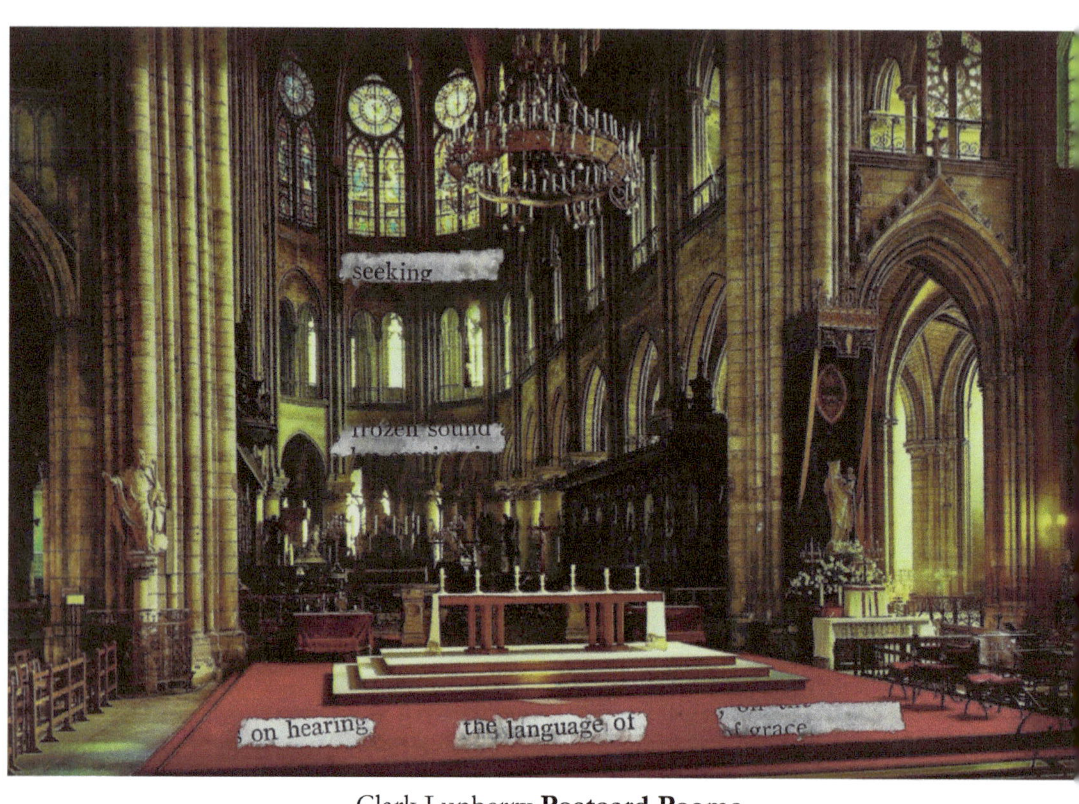

Clark Lunberry **Postcard Poems**

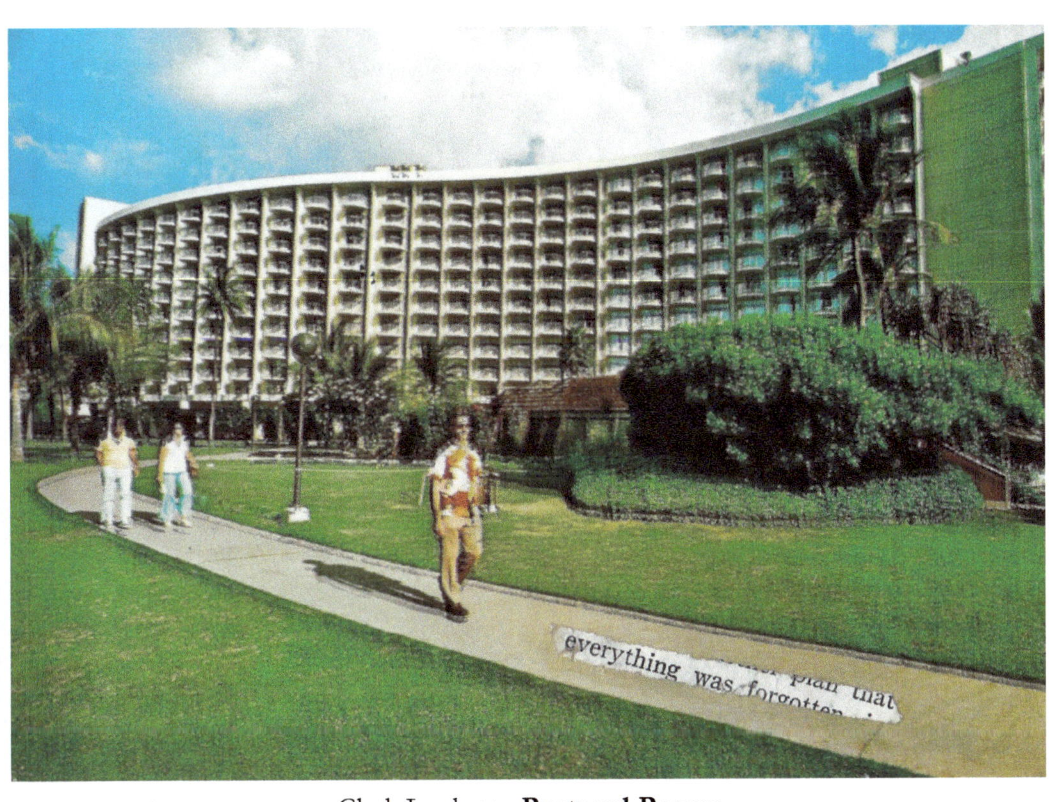

Clark Lunberry **Postcard Poems**

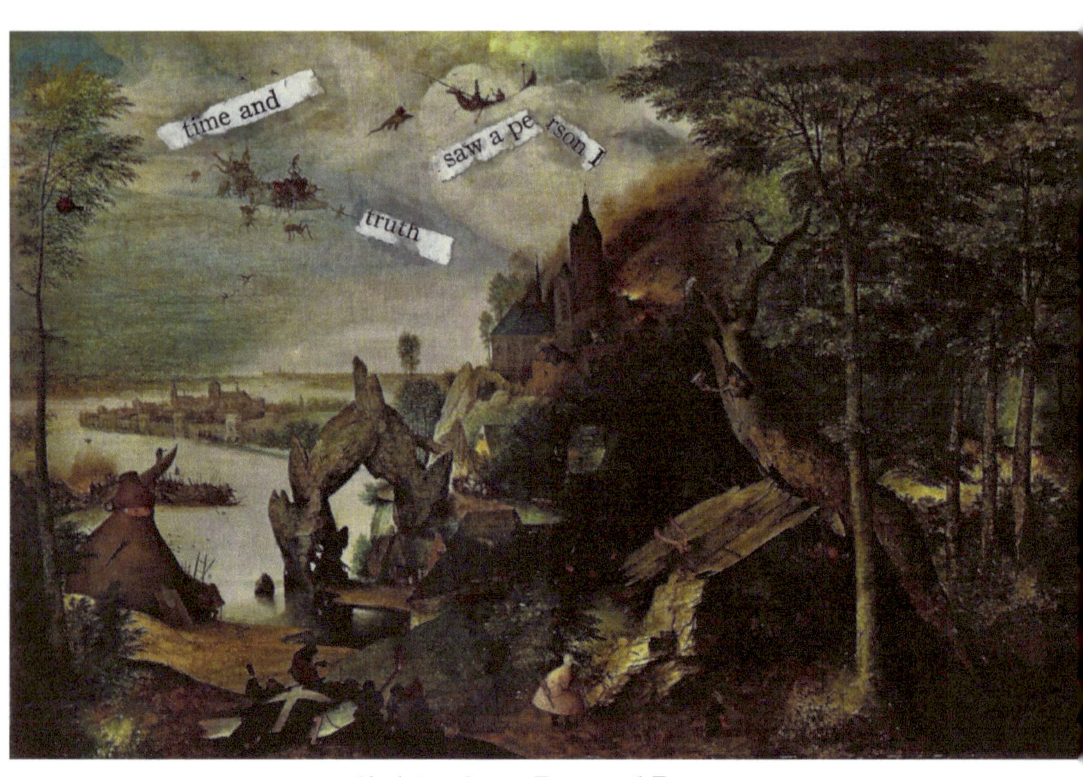

Clark Lunberry **Postcard Poems**

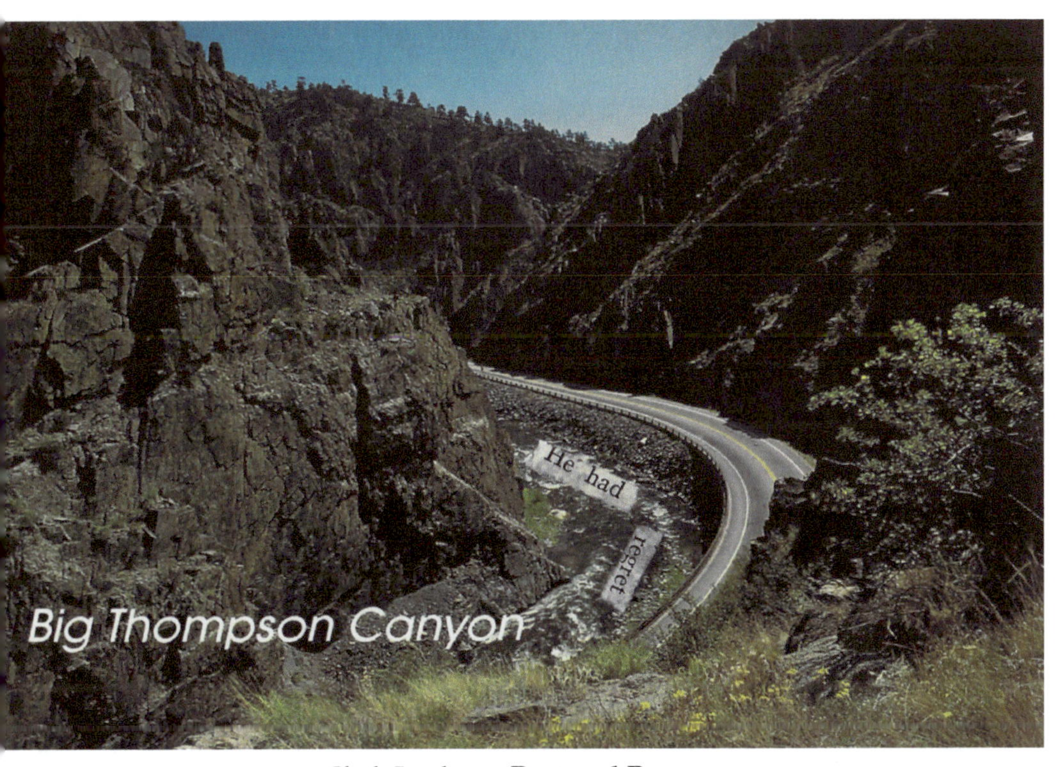

Clark Lunberry **Postcard Poems**

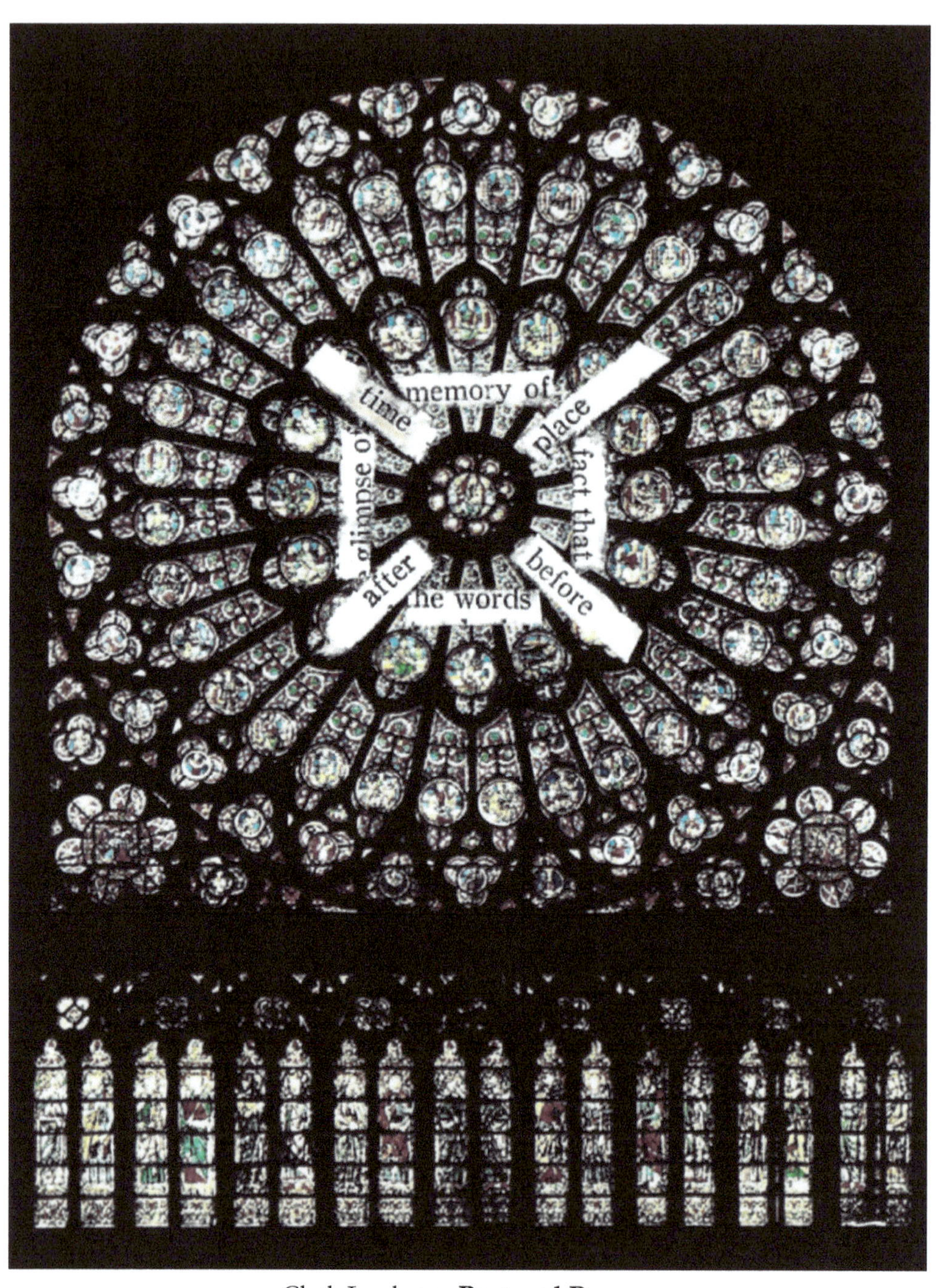

Clark Lunberry **Postcard Poems**

Gordon Blitz
Piles of Matter

Scraps of the day
Go to the compost
Recycling words that
Can be grown
Into an organic truth
That would have been wasted
In brainy landfills
Taking up mindful space
Preventing the raw browns and greens
From being released
Particles of carbon and nitrogen
Combined with moisture
To break down the looping

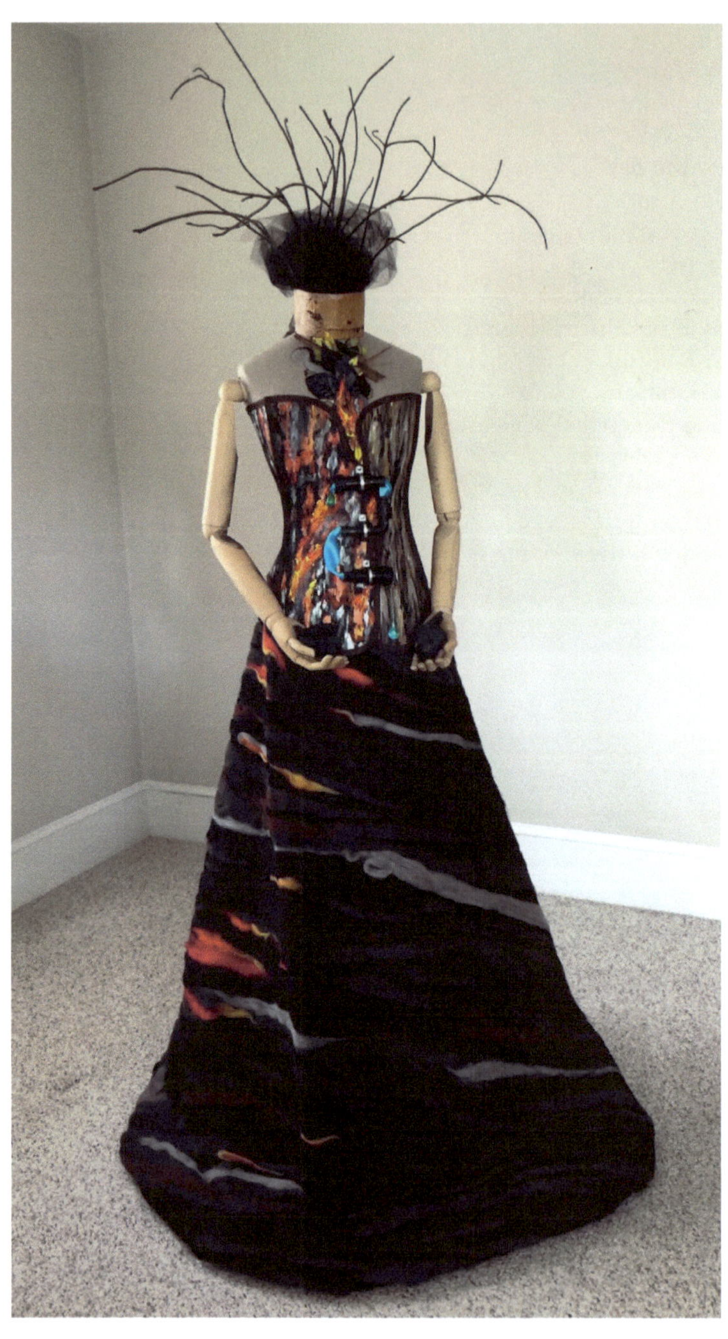

Cynthia Kerby
**Wildfires/Megafires/Flashpoint: Crossing a New Threshold.
Binding Consequences without Constraints**

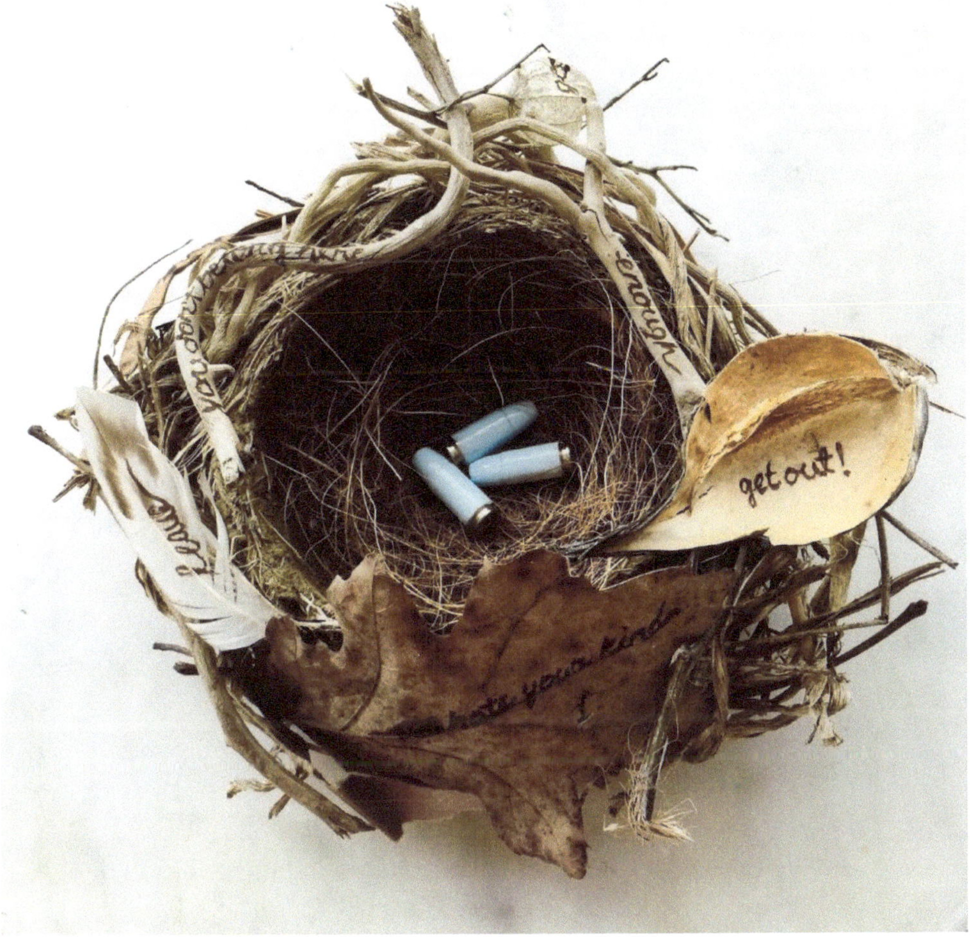

Cynthia Kerby
Nested Homegrown Beliefs:
Observing Incubations of Intolerance

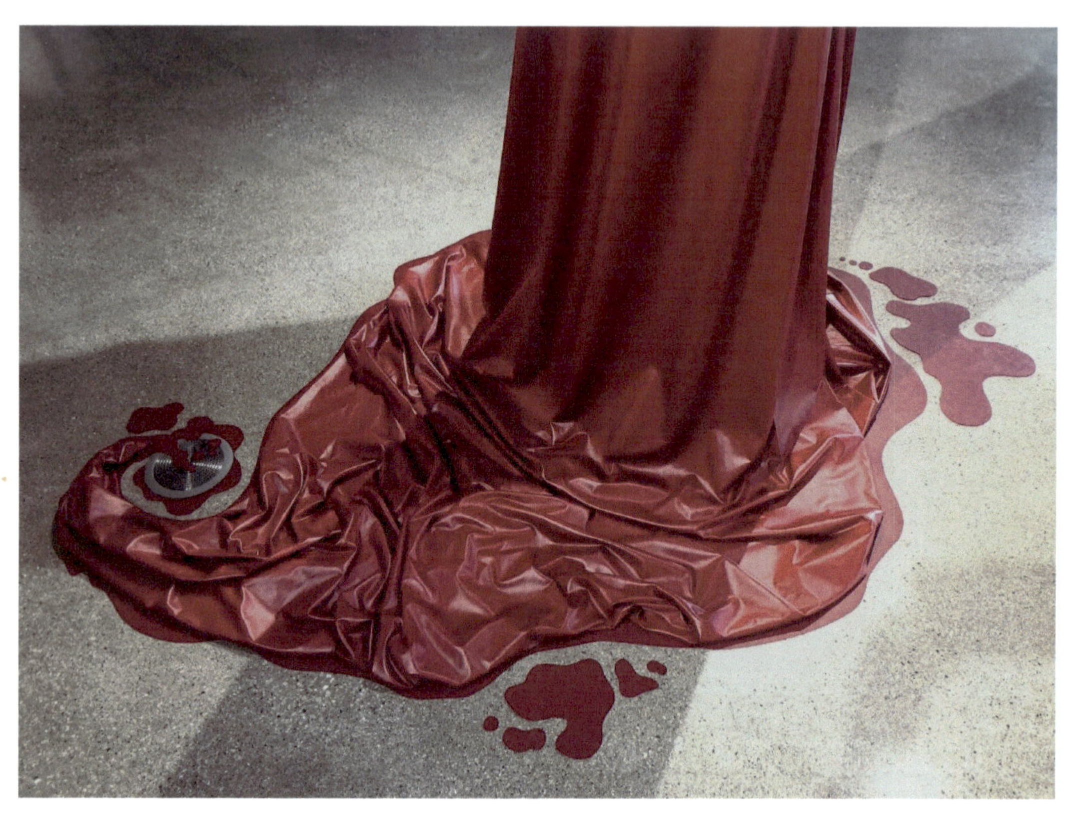

Cynthia Kerby
Low Tide/High Tide/Red Tide: Our New Binding Reality. The Constraints of Consequence

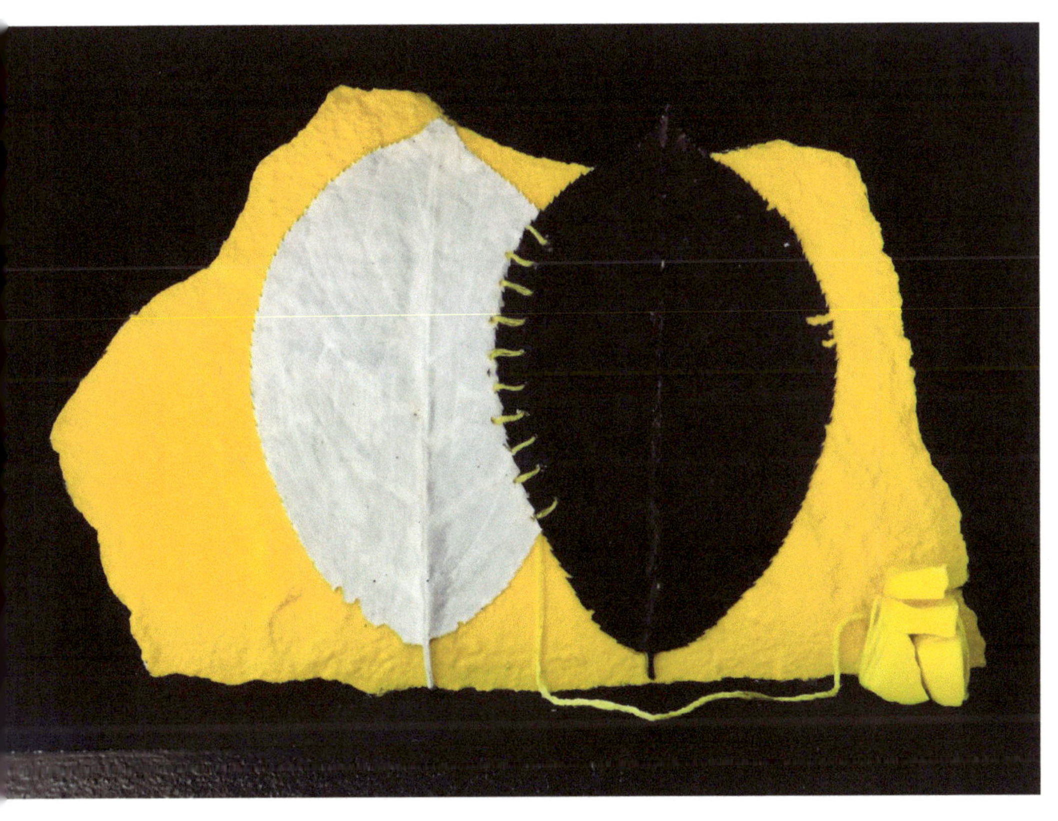

Cynthia Kerby
Deconstruct/Reconstruct Change

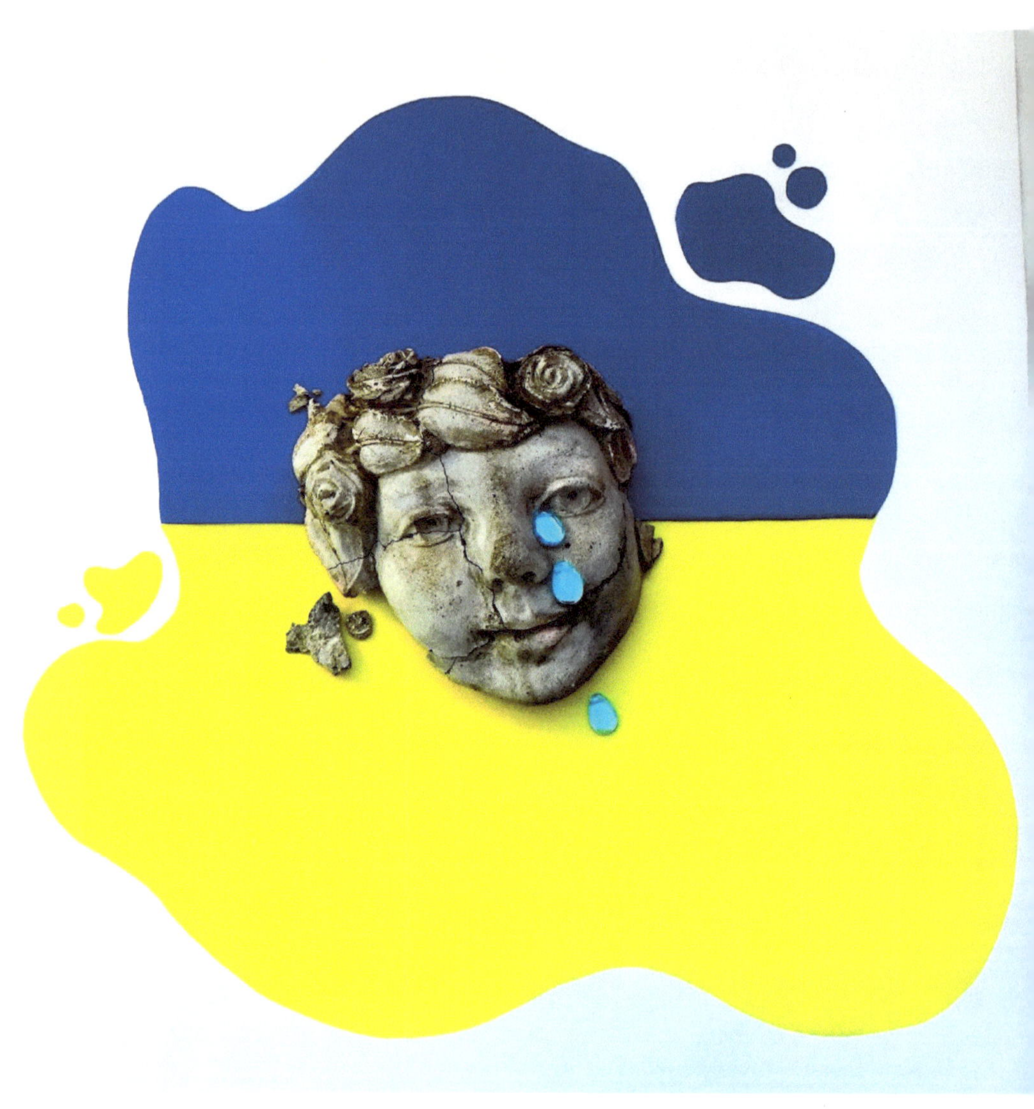

Cynthia Kerby **Mending the Spoils of War**

Ignatius Valentine Aloysius & Brian L. Jacobs
AS THE WORLD RISES FROM A CHILL

the dewy light lights transgress root

tremble in definitions exile

blackened pink in the ash'd heap

bosom'd in semantic turfs   mingling

heart fire fuel, daily fines.

                                     can you

imagine Heaven's first morning, wrought

green gold   crown of pardons, those

dewy heights incessantly blind?

Ignatius Valentine Aloysius & Brian L. Jacobs
VAST LIBRARIES

abutting a catalogue
of fixed forms

affectation
or coquetry

lips
of earth—

The tense ahead of one of us
intensifies its stock

of language forms
dancing in our

throats, saying
"understand me!" I am

sorghum thread
sugar bump fertility bunts   sparsely

settled steps >
we are not Einsatzgruppe

bearing peace cranes not scepters
as we eat at your salt bread and dance

in the rich mineral orbits
of ice ponds   bookshelves

six suns bright   us
at perfect will > perfecting

what must be salved or
returned this week. Refused!

Listening awkwardly
dictated moons

adumbrated hymens
the parallax of my loins misunderstood

by their preying-mantis
business, sharpened teeth

weighing too-old experiments
kept running farther

chasing a future of   tofu & milk
& so whom should we trust?

Ignatius Valentine Aloysius & Brian L. Jacobs
SLOW REVOLUTIONS OF THE PEN BEYOND WARTIME

          But where is the cutting edge?
You'll have to have a leg blown off in Ukraine to be somebody

while gold tall grasses weep and torn grain silos spill despair
blood red on the Western gridiron, this wordless sun

cum chews Renaissance bent down towards broken feet
upside down azaleas bloom in rupture's beauty sin the adverse day complete

and yet the cutting edge shies, fingers pointing towards
the great enterprise and mother's pleased friends, prisoners all

in the othersphere rhizomatically wheat'd in acumen blistered edge   cutting
geometric and Michaelangelo'd in this gridiron communion'd pilgrimage

liberating heart and torment, commandeered sums of relief seizing
runaway multiplicities reaching for burning vessels, mosaics, bodies.

Art prepared us for war   Tulip'd rouge bilboes between toes gather
valved in the presses of words abandon

-ing shame, abandoning the cold imposed morality of gunmetal sin
while tool's rebellion blades rise in ascension against   war's raw disease—

Pure the kiss kiss in the dermis memory
the time of your own think schist comets in the un hum drum

lets the sun come through brightly, forging flattery in shadow's palaces
and running sacred the cutting edge so blissful along Adam's apple

shifts shifts in the dogma   Avalanche
Eve's eve dawn the prior liberator of your berry purple

revolution   lifts all wealth, wheat stalks, the poisoned pen scuttling towards
its maker's mark & continents of language missed through seasons' frosts

balanced on history cuff
never again never again never again.

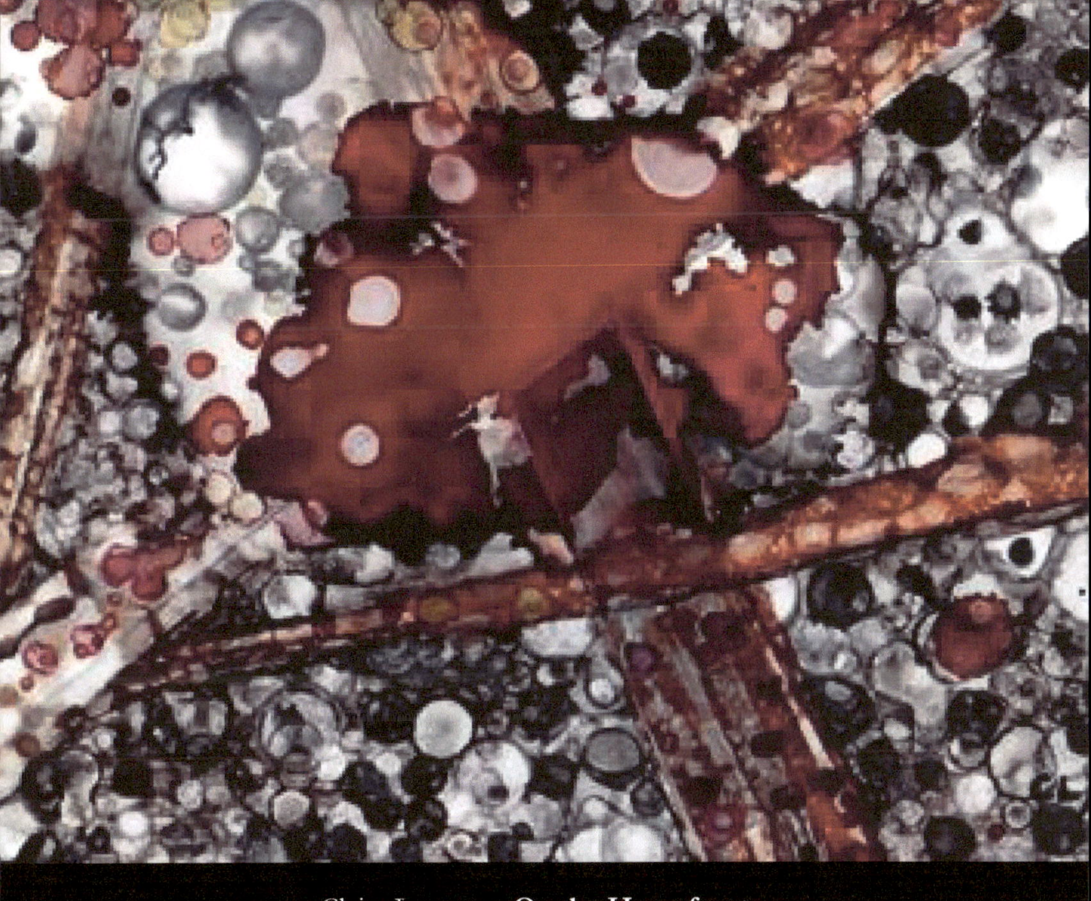

Claire Lawrence **On the Homefront**

Brian Yapko
For the Children

The sculpted outlines of a hawk
and a hare In the heat of afternoon
both panting in the shade of a juniper.
Alert, the raptor dissembles — she

preens her feathers as the mammal hides
trembling in a field sniffing at the air. The
duet-duel of dancing limbs and creature
noises salts the windless doldrums.

All at once broken branches and a flurry
of dislodged needles beats percussion into
blood and life consumes itself like a
mandala, painstaking but temporary.

They death-mate, heard but unseen,
behind the red clay where the boulders grow.
One mother's child is given to another
mother's child as the sun turns its face

and the clouds ignore the fading pleas.
Must it be? the child asks, eyes wide.
The mother answers, I do not know.
But this is how it has always been done.

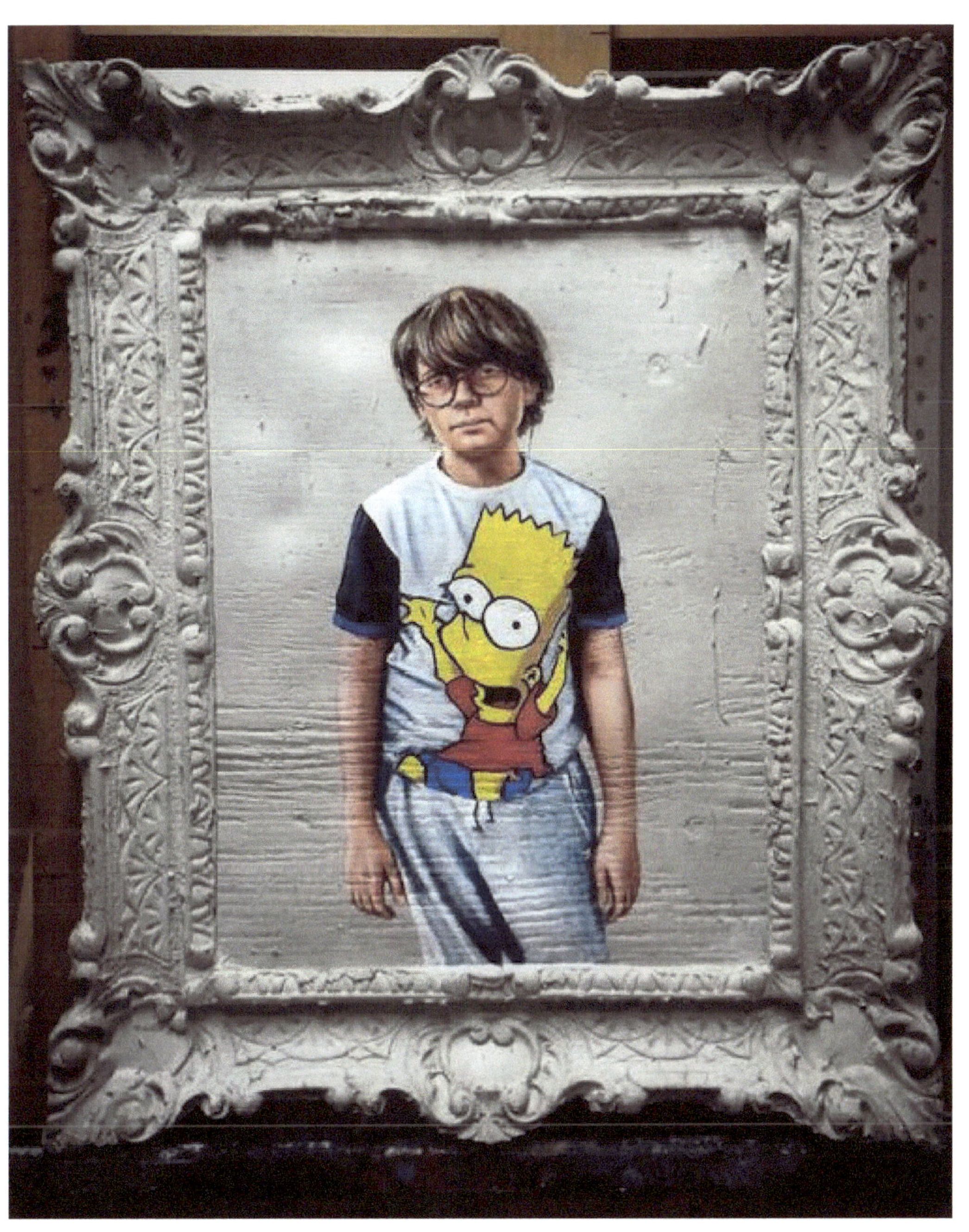

Mario Loprete **FRANCESCO** Oil on Concrete 50 cm x 60 cm

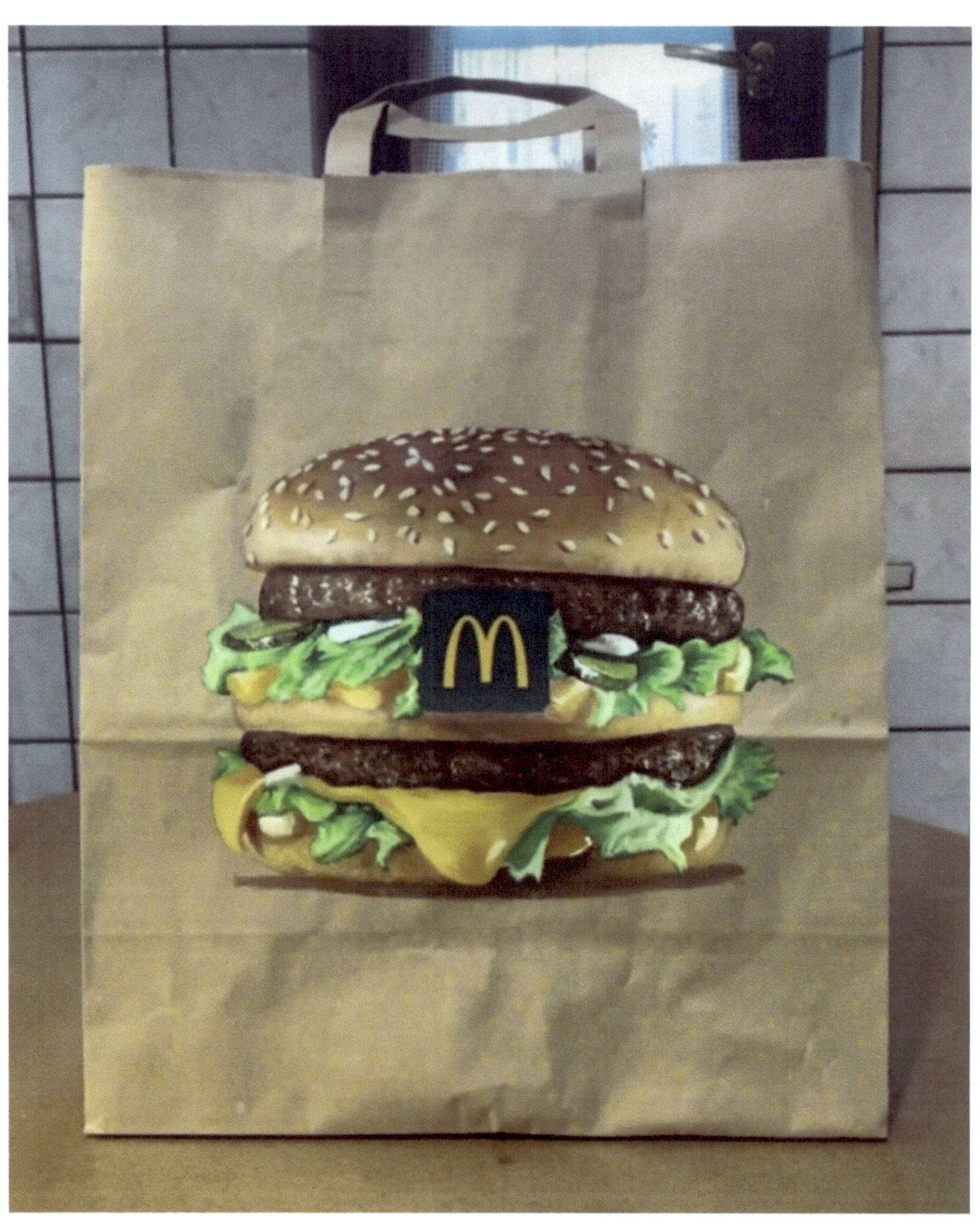

Mario Loprete **MC Mario** Oil on McDonald's Cardboard Bag

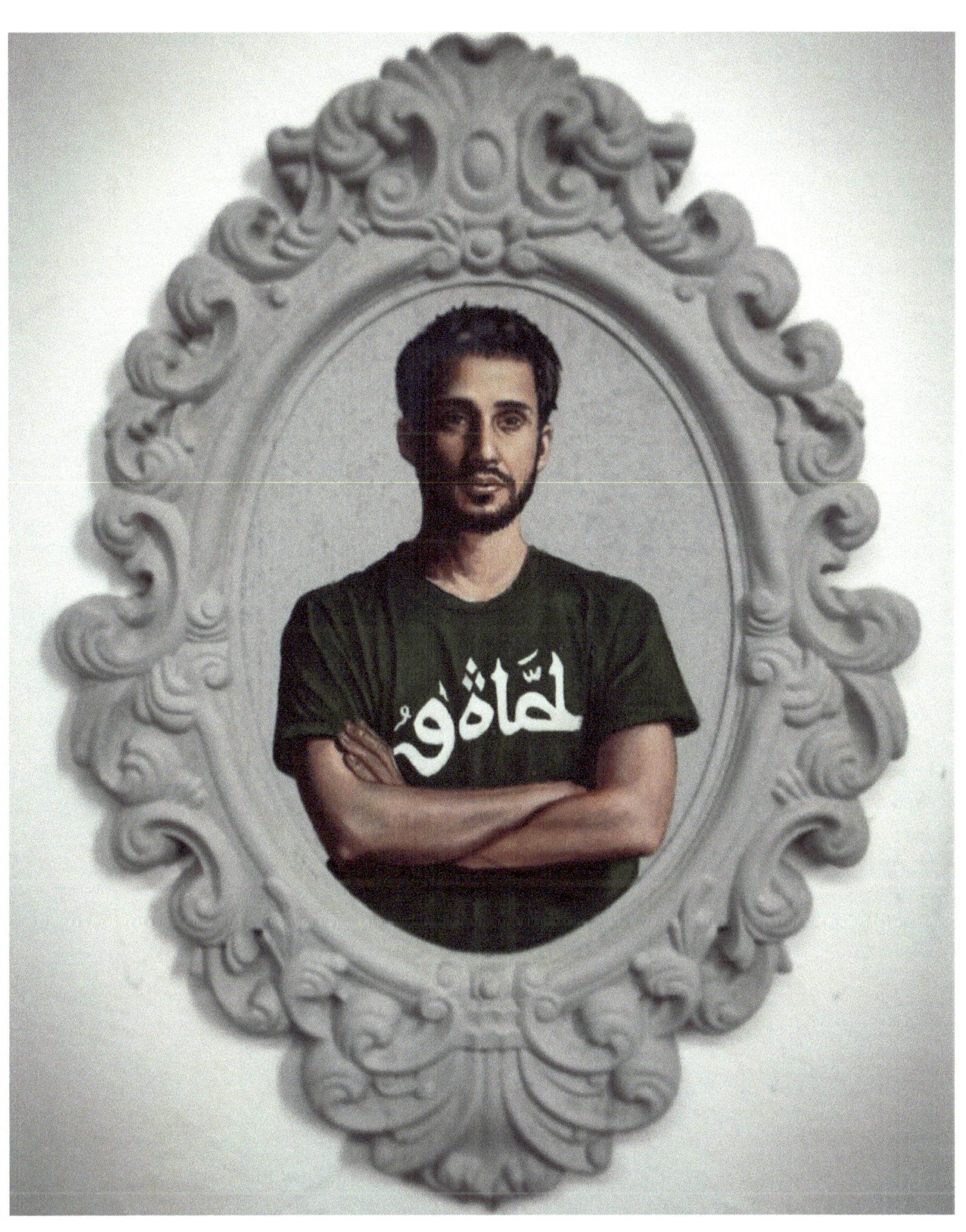

Mario Loprete **B-BOY** Oil on Concrete 30 cm x 40 cm

Amy Lerman
Urban Legend

That day when the sun trellises
the sidewalk and your fingers crumple,
then re-crumple a straw's wrapper,
the friend you haven't seen since before
tells you how they still need to write
the letter, the donor years below
the registry lady's assurance of age
27 the night she called to offer
a kidney, to save a husband's life.

Unlike a sitcom scene where
the expectant father grabs the prepacked
hospital suitcase for his contracting
wife, your friend will describe measured
chaos—three hours to call someone
to dog sit because the standbys
are out of town; to repackage half
a "before bed" edible; to stop
for gas before the 40-minute drive
to life.

He is better now, your friend
will smile, the recovery slow
but there, her head seeming
involuntary in its shaking
and lowering, as she will tell you
of their gratefulness and how
hollow she feels, she didn't
expect this need
to restrain from cringing
at well-wishers' *It's a miracle*,
her thoughts constant
to the family who has lost
a daughter, the Rudolph antlers
she wore every Christmas morning
muddled with Little League softball
trophies shelved in the garage;
grandchildren she never bore; a
blond ponytail; her insides

and you will feel the guilt transplant,
behind your nods and shared tears,
your mind will picture the bathtub
of ice, an immersed body coming
to consciousness and note--
"Your kidneys are gone. Call 911"--
written by strangers from a previous
night's party, could this be the donor's
fate? you simultaneously will consider
and chide over the impossibility,
so much water melting, overflowing,
drowning moments away.

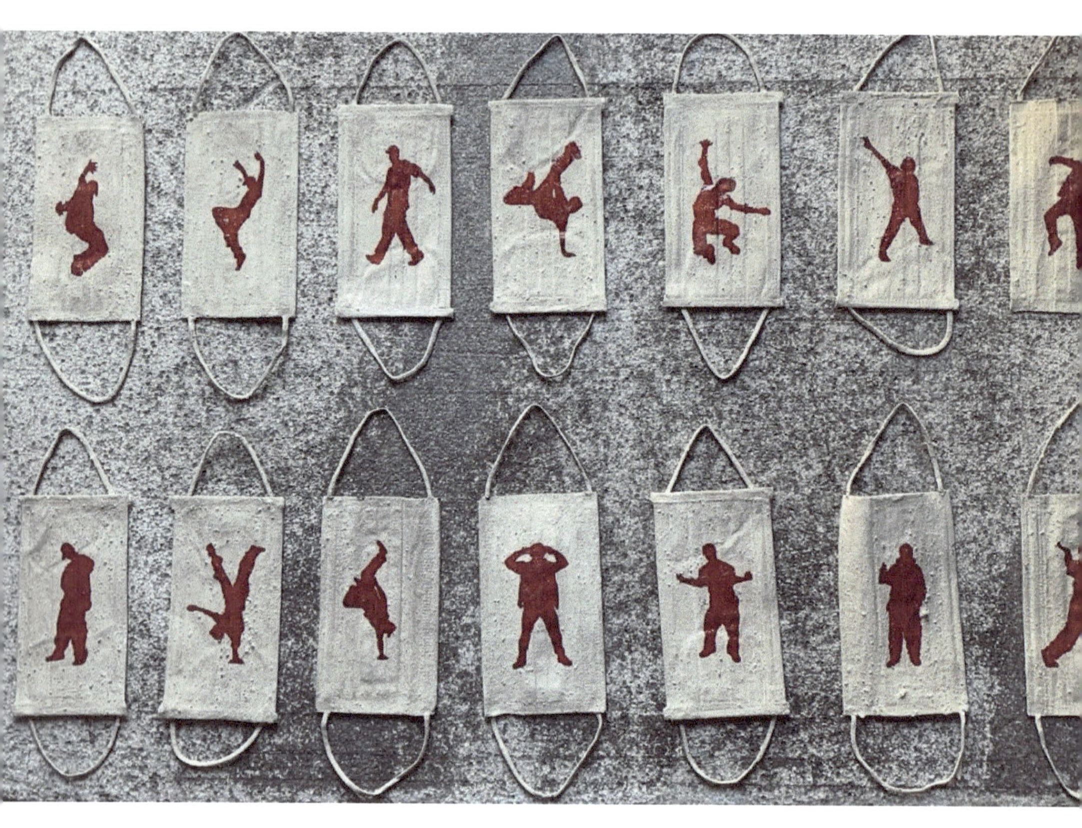

Mario Loprete **FUCKOVID** Enamel and Cement on Surgical Masks

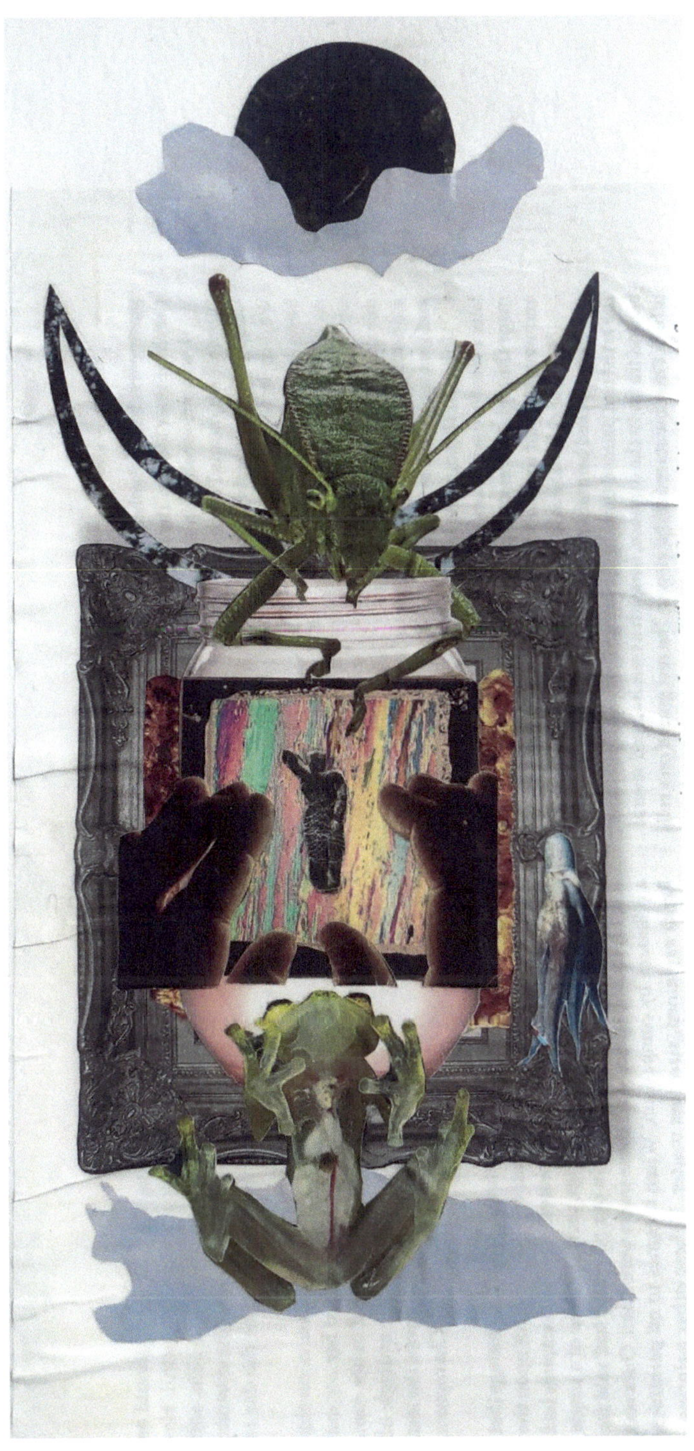

R.L. Edmondson Vance **DIY Goddess, collage, 2019**

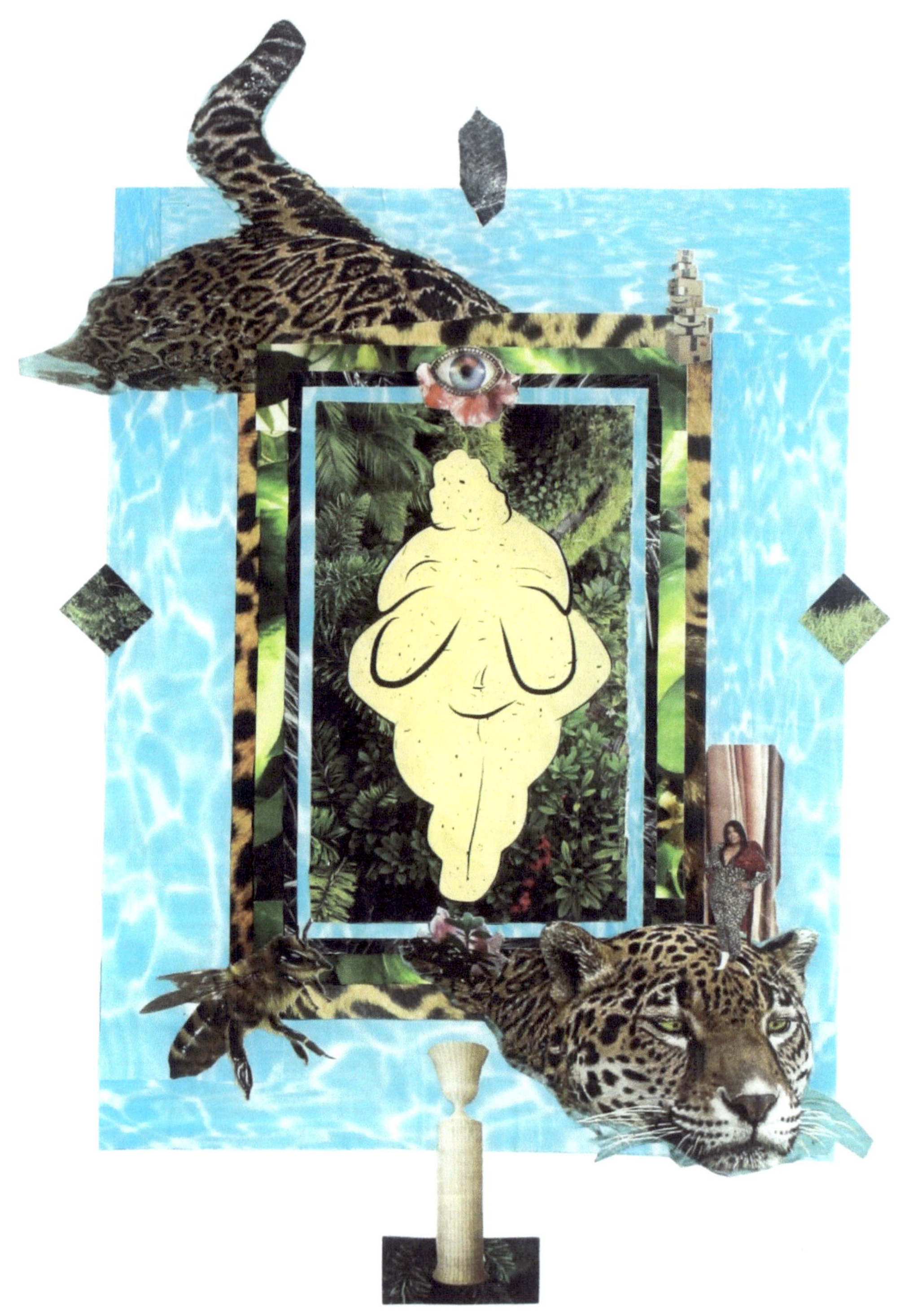

R.L. Edmondson Vance **Night Light Goddess, Collage 2019**

Jones Irwin
Moira
'A hell of a woman' – Jim Thompson

I
Let me tell that tragi-comic tale once more
the fast-talking shower of queers
no words just desires and drives.
Wasn't Moira the queen of them gangsters?
Worser she was they said
especially in that King-sized bed of hers.
Through the long bleak Seventies
she kept a feral house of strays
had no qualm with seeing a few slip away
if necessary. Wasn't she meant to have popped
old Grisly Irish Raymond with her very own hands?
They say she finished him with a claw hammer

bashed his ugly brains out all over the bar table
the commotion spilling the gang's collection of beer
into the interstitial space of O'Hara's exposed frontal lobes.
Looked like a Pollock, or worser a Freud, Francis Bacon laughed
in the *Coach and Horses* after in between gin Martini pints
this bunch of neo-Action Painters making startling order
out of supposed chaos in Soho even if to the untrained a mess.

Nothing boring anyhows, ain't that right? Gangsters are sure vivid.
Moira loved it lapped it up the minutes and the bloody seconds
of evil excitement. Their trembling fear her power her pleasure
getting her sexy long stockinged legs over the prettier
Eton Harries. That chunky long leopard skin coat as a signature.
No years in domestic hell or the clink for her
myriad extortion or murder cases taken out well before

they got anywhere near somewhere
like court. Crooked cops. Death's sister.

II
Suppose you could
file her under *sociopath*
going way beyond the individual
with her set of intersubjective cronies
a whole Middlesex mini universe of cut-throat
this and that hard against the loftier values
sown into the fabric of post-War life.

Iconoclast then though not sure
she or hers stand for anything
or if there was an underlying
project of any kind other than
greed and mayhem from the very
get-go probably kicked-off with
that Clacton-On-Sea heist which went
badly wrong and they had to finish
the bravely resistant postmistress who had
already seen too much.

Now we have all seen way too much
but these days there can be no going back.

III

Flashing her bristols was Moira. *Do
you ever wonder*, she asked, *where
the bodies go?* The liquid slap of the head
as they died. One last oh soundful
so sorrowful sigh. That incongruous stare
without any care not even looking over
her shoulder. I tryin' hard shoot elsewhere
suggested the countryside. Anyhows I'd been
thinking more about the souls after death, like.

*Out somewhere in the sticks?
Nah fool boy*, she said, *not there. Where
then?* Her bristols all pricked up now like
she was gettin' extra-excited. In her deep V
you were lost you could well see
she had plenty of what it took. *Really don't knows
where. Why does it matter? Nowhere
maybe.* She laughs. *Where's that baby?* That hot
red lipstick made her lips Satanic. Nowhere

did exist. I had been there. Years before
I remembered. Dark place more
sweaty than rock n' roll fever. Music deeper and
scarier. She was biting the quiver on her
lower lip now. *Wanna be lovers*,
she asked? *Moira*, I said, *yea sure.*

IV
Worst decision ever. Woman means
you no harm her other boyos had said.
A soft spot there. Not to be believed.
Could show you the snuff video tapes if I
was allowed to keep 'em. Lucky
to be still alive only cos I kept my
mouth shut. Pusface. Plus
eyes. Past is no window only
a painting you gotta interpret or last
night's performance you gotta forget. I
was never very good at sleeping soundly or
at understanding pure malice. Weak me, eh?

So off you go East London mate out
towards Plaistow so as
to read the concrete prose. Biblical.
There, you can read the graffiti
smells like piss. At least it's real.
At least it is real like evil. Carnal.
Learn your life lesson. Then move on.
If you possibly can.

V
Then again, maybe trouble never wants
to move on. Maybe you cannot.
Highlight the survivor bit.
Won't let yourself. Remember Gisèle
that woman what happened her.
Hate has its reasons. Also Laima
from Lithuania not Vilnius
but Kaunas. The smaller second city.
Some faces you cannot ever forget.
Disappeared one night by Moira
and by her men. We all knew.
The worst kind of slowly delayed end.
That one gave me running nightmares.
Pregnant remains on a bonfire.
What could we do?
Didn't find out until after
of course. 'Wise intervened.

Jones Irwin
A Superior Inner Life

The bedroom

was pale pink

and had the look

of a superior

inner life insofar

as no attention had

been paid to order, whatsoever.

Jones Irwin
Debord and Christ

Mid-week, mid-term
You could read *Inherent Vice*
And see if you can sense
The beach beneath
The paving stones

Lying on the pathway
In central Leeds
Imagining the sea spray
Backwash on your face
You are stripped near-naked
And all the locals
Are somewhat taken aback

It's your candour which
I find most a shock
Says one a collared
Minister who seems
To make the link finally
Between Debord and Christ

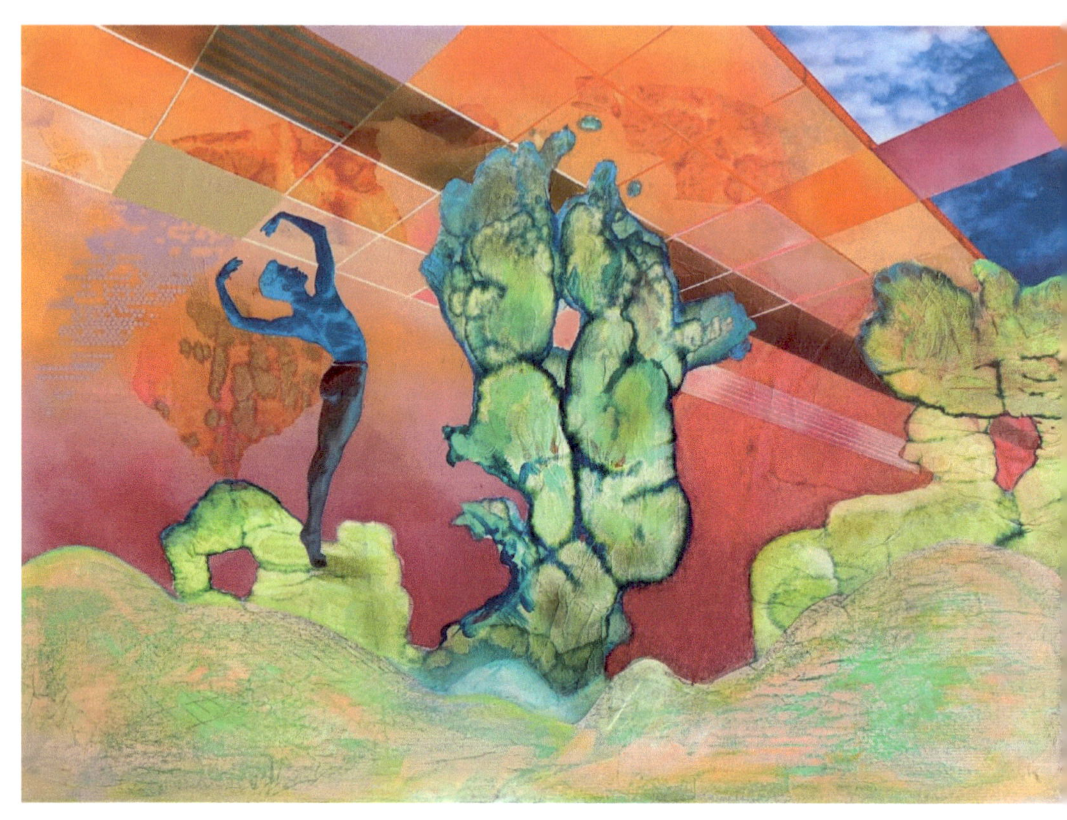

Abol Bahadori **Skylight Dream**

Karin Falcone Krieger
The Night Gave Us Ice

1.
An ice storm was blowing toward Millay
so the wisest thing to do was stay
I dreamt of Canada and then it came
ice covered this forest, every tree
the colorless day revealed a path
that yesterday had not occurred to me
cracking the ice-over-snow with my boots
like a spoon cracks sugar on crème brulee.

I pause to listen
the whole sky hissing and spitting like a kitten
sharp claw needles hit my face
trees take a bow and break out loud
dead wood pruned by act of God.

Raspberry canes bend to the ground
glass around their frozen crowns
where fall held golden promise
and winter shut it down.

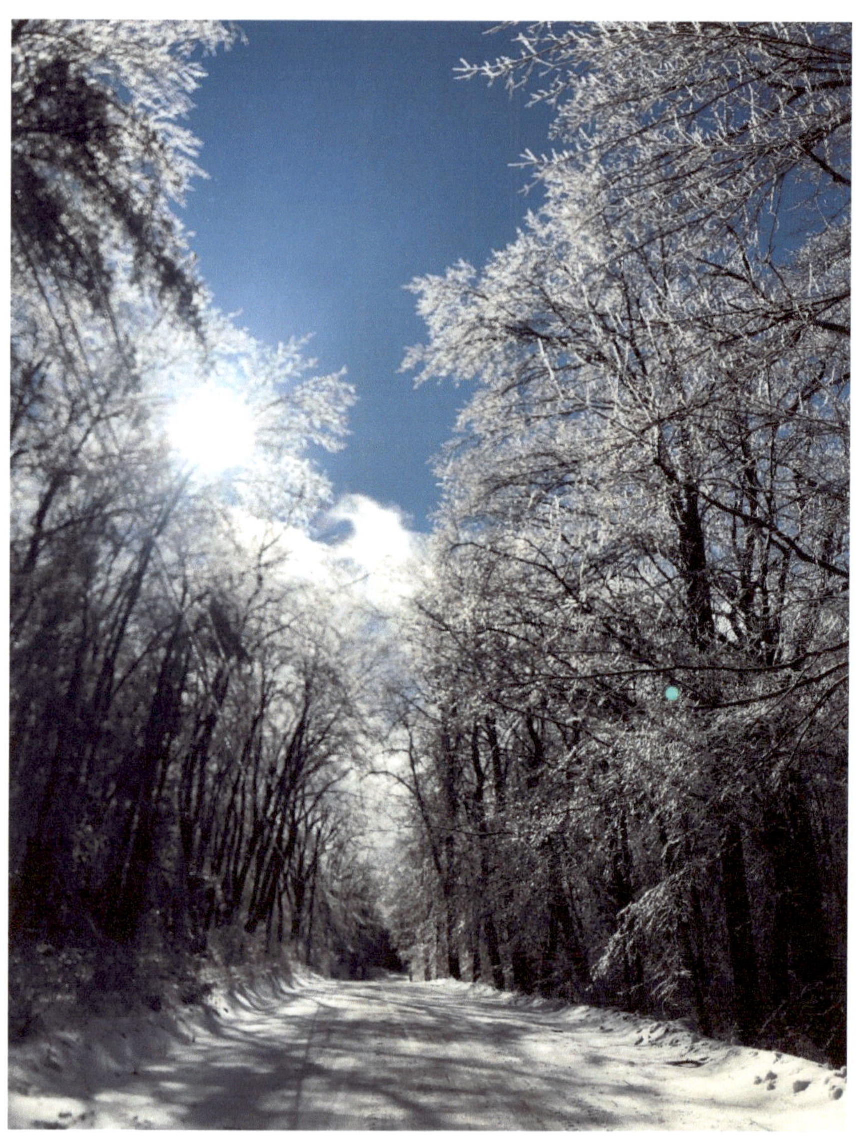

2.
Snows came blowing in like sands
far below zero in late afternoon
everything turned blue like a glacier crevasse
the color a girl in a princess dress
in a snow globe would imagine for you.
The north wind white and night fall purple
a planet like this, a world impossible.

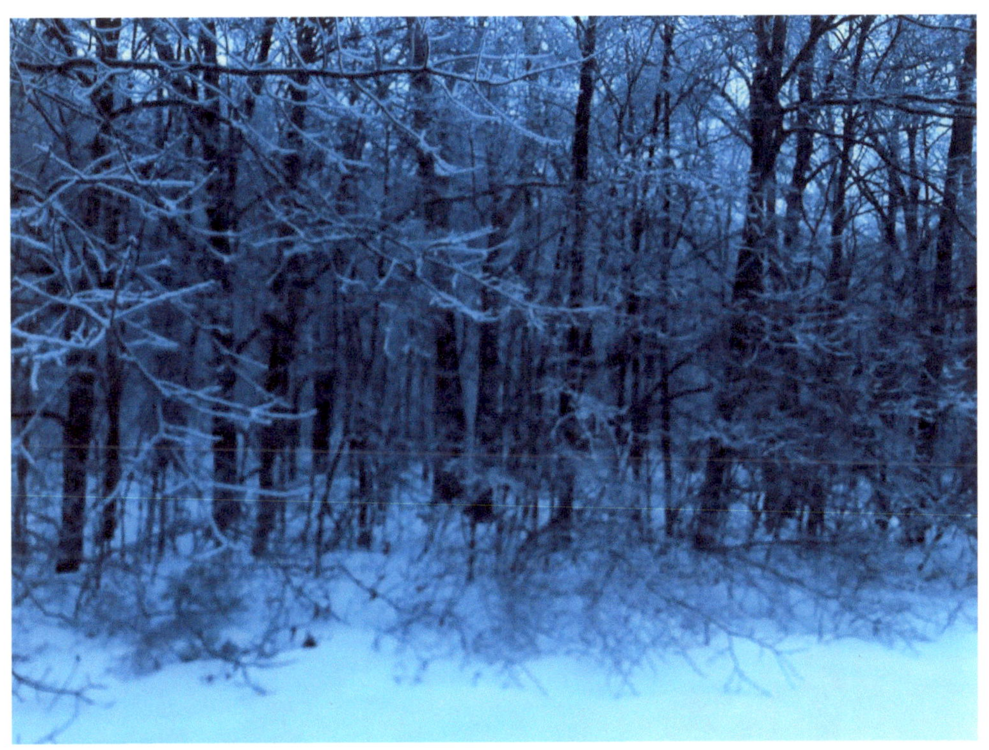

3.
The second morning I see from bed
snow rise and fly of its own volition
like a swarm of gnats awakened by June
a short film in negative
white flies, new moon

The second morning was like falling in love
after a late-night hook up obsessed
wet beauty done deed afterglow at last
time slows as mercury drops
freeze frame of a time before past

Burdened black trees still sway
wearing wind chimes made of prisms
as the clouds move away.
I take photographs on Candlemas
a poor Lucite re-creation
falsified Yuletide postcard mission
winter's desire to hold something wild
grapples with the groundhog's decision.

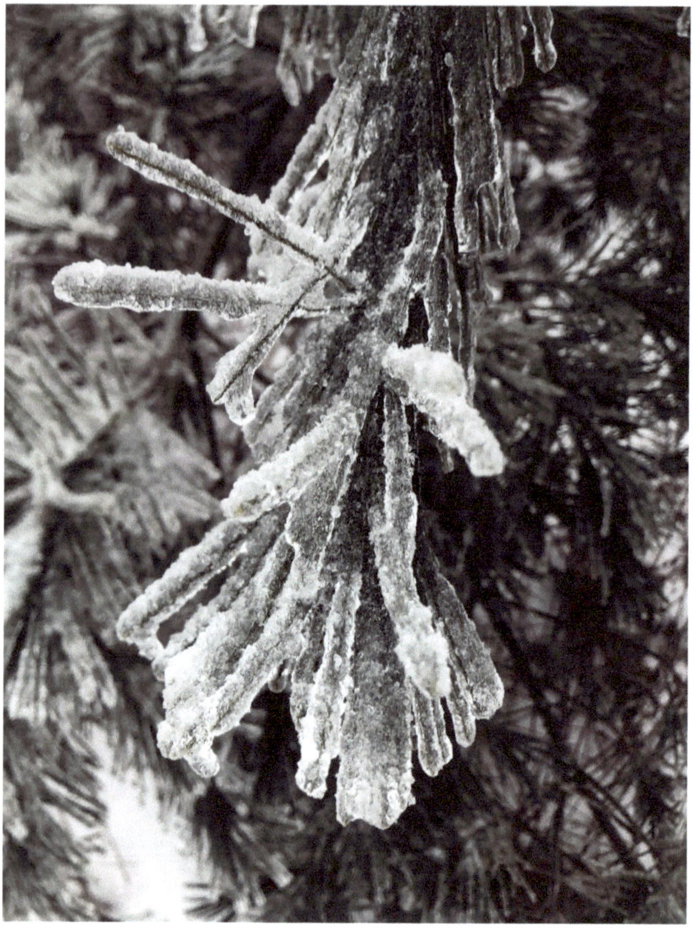

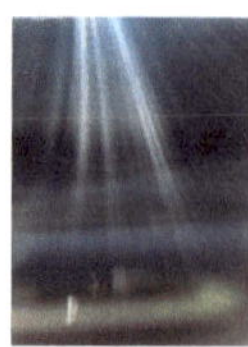

4.
I mix up my days in the rising sun.
Who would not be wildly or mildly interested
in the ephemeral multi-media work of a briefly
visiting artist known as Ice Storm?
Rainbow points at every angle
the pink green flash of a visiting angel
I hold pieces of shattered pine
as I strive to take my leave
and snow devils circle my feet in the drive.

Brendan Lorber
The best stories are what you get out of

The best stories   are what you get   out of getting into the worst jams
I don't mean to play up   the cavernous glamour   of abandoned
terminals   reclaimed to get it on   with the dewy acquisition
of my own tics and manners   that were others' first   Nobody does
that   or means to   justify the recursive clamor   of the undying
dawn drawn jetset   with horn rims and pearls   which did for then
what the unknown   tropes of our moment   are doing   if not
to us   then to the precociously belated off-brand nuzzle   we cast
a hopeful eye   to a pet or foxy neighbor for   This despite the belief
in science   and sell-by dates   on shrines lit from within   a different
era   a kind of gate   in the distance   designed to be held open
past   the final boarding call's   almost inaudible announcement
that the arrow of cupid   or maybe the sharper one of time   zeros
in   but not which one   aloft in the wake of our curated affairs

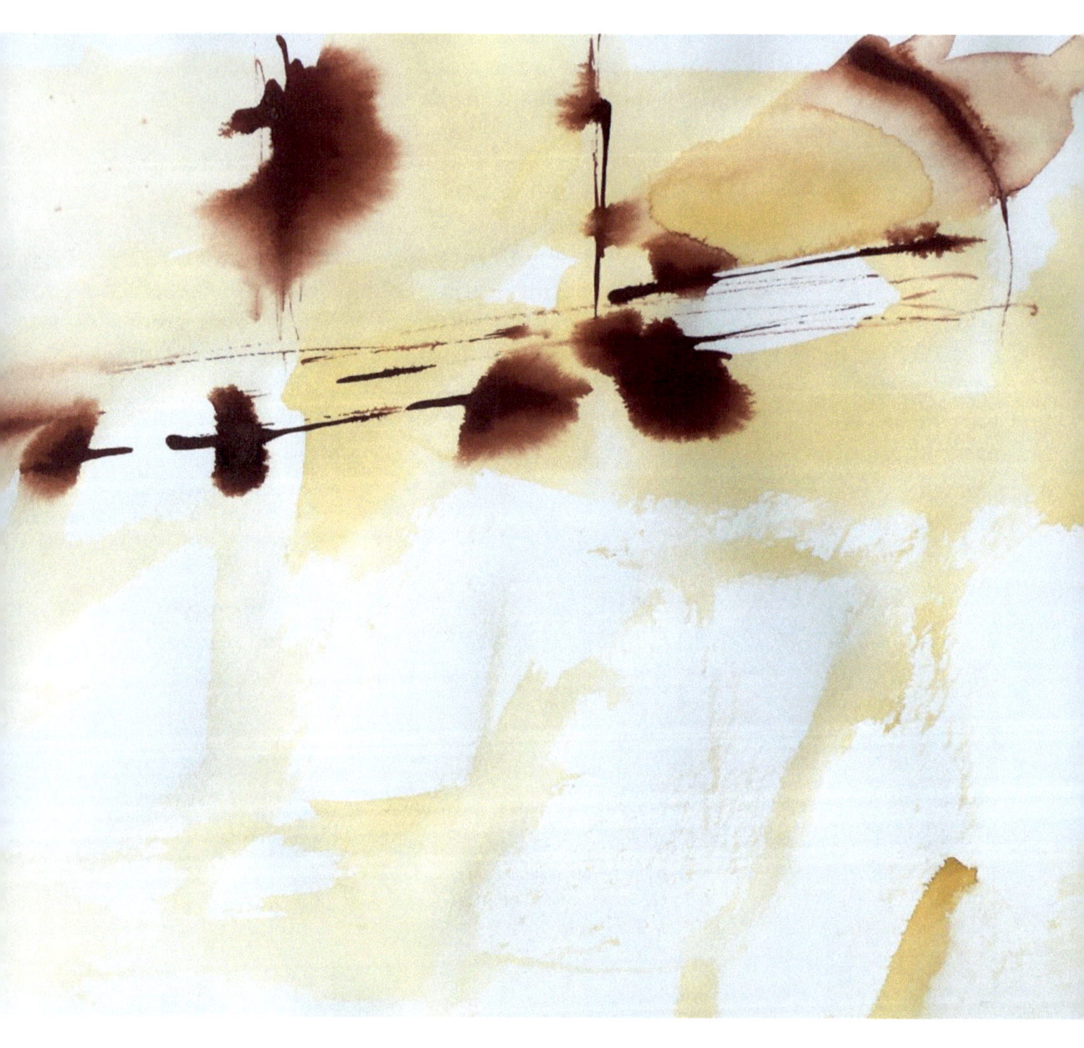

Aaron Hoge **Lover's Leap Bridge**

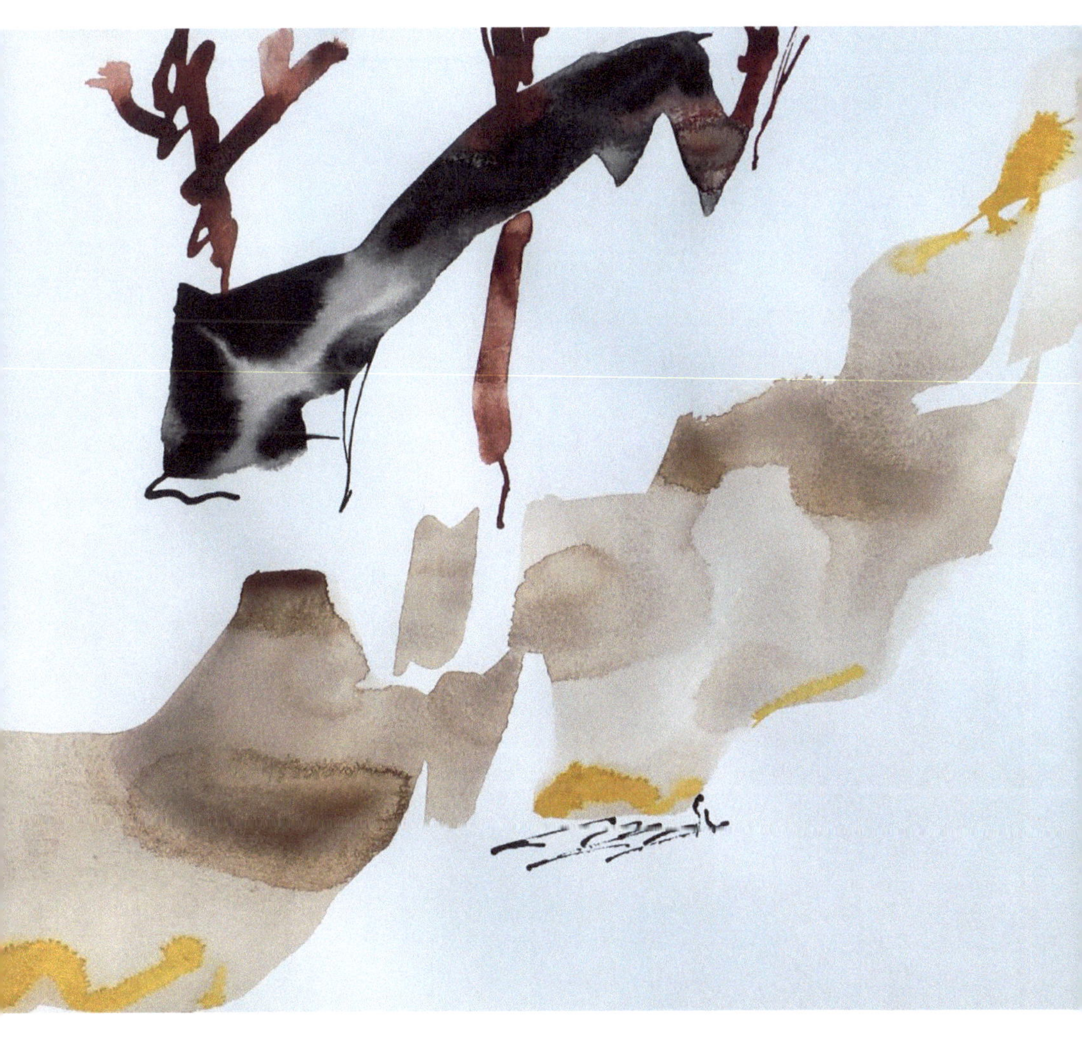

Aaron Hoge **The Stone Wall**

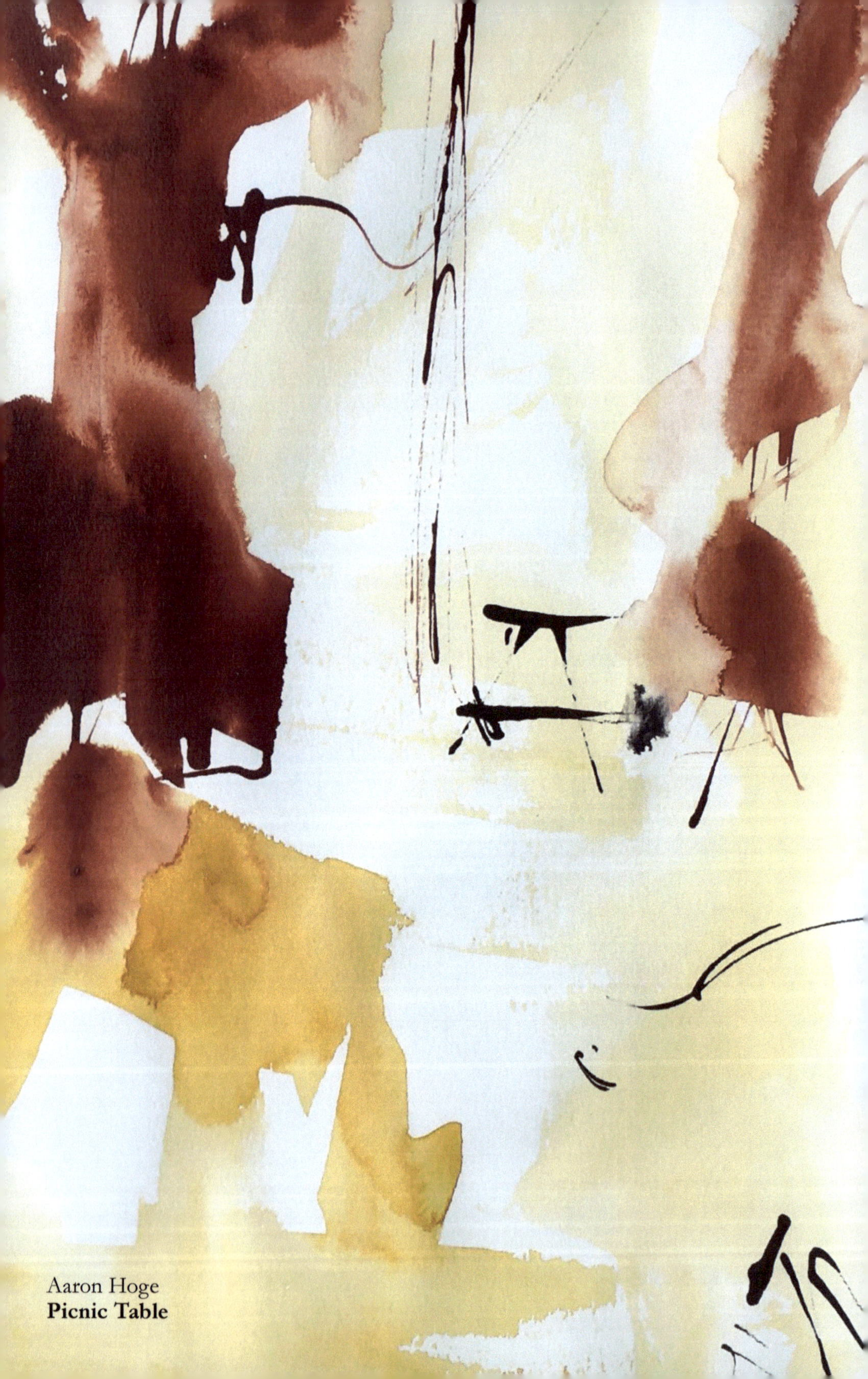

Aaron Hoge
Picnic Table

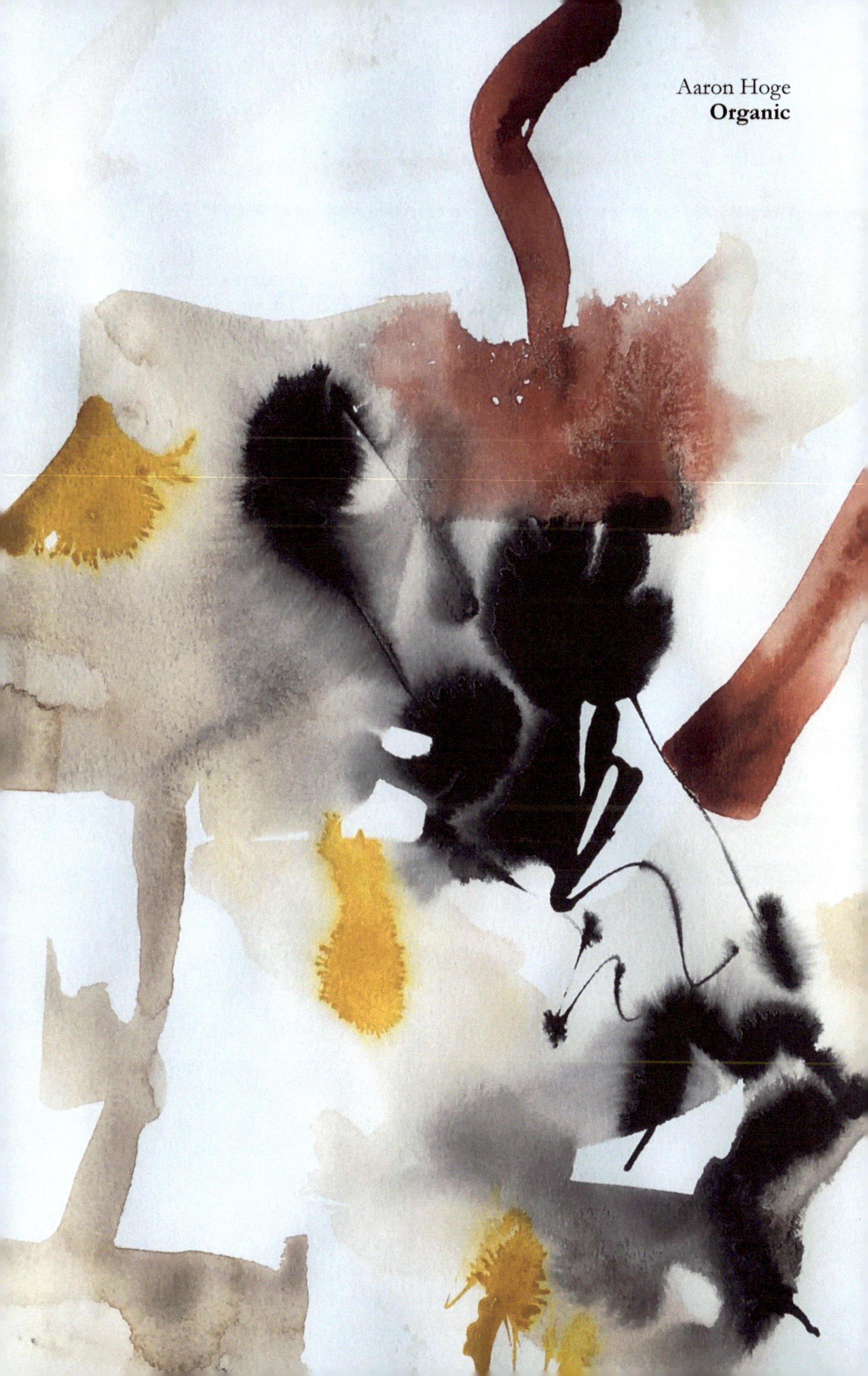
Aaron Hoge
Organic

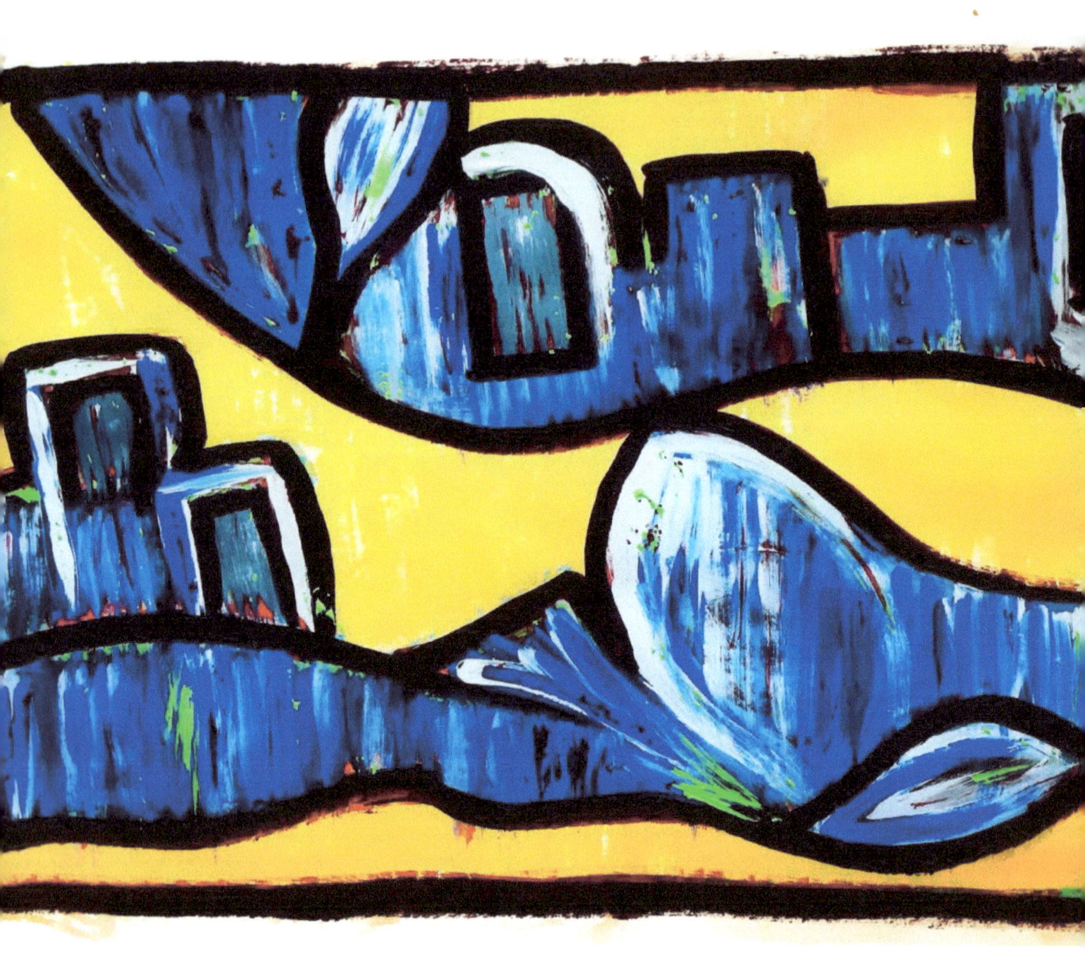

Aaron Hoge **Imaginary Landscapes**

Charles Becker
What We Learn In School

It was third grade when I started having crushes
on other boys. No one knew. My very first
fascination came with Steve J. in the classroom
next to mine. He was popular, athletic, strong.
I stole quick looks at his handsome, symmetrical
face so he wouldn't catch me. His hands were
big. When our classes played softball, he was
always the captain, pitcher, umpire. He knew
everything about sports and how his body
worked. As teams chose sides and best batters,
I was always picked right before the quiet, delicate
girls. We were last but had each other and together
tried to avoid embarrassment in front of our heart-
throb. We didn't have much skill yet, especially
not me, naming any true feelings. But I remember
the day my words finally came. Our school was
having a spelling bee and Steve's class, challenging
mine, brought their own chairs into my room.
We all squeezed close together. Even though Steve
didn't wind up next to me, it was close enough
for me to see he was wearing new cowboy boots,
boots that shined with masculinity and design.
He was happier and more popular than before,
and I understood all at once that I would never
be brave enough to talk to him, and I would never,
ever be able to wear cowboy boots with such certainty
and poise.

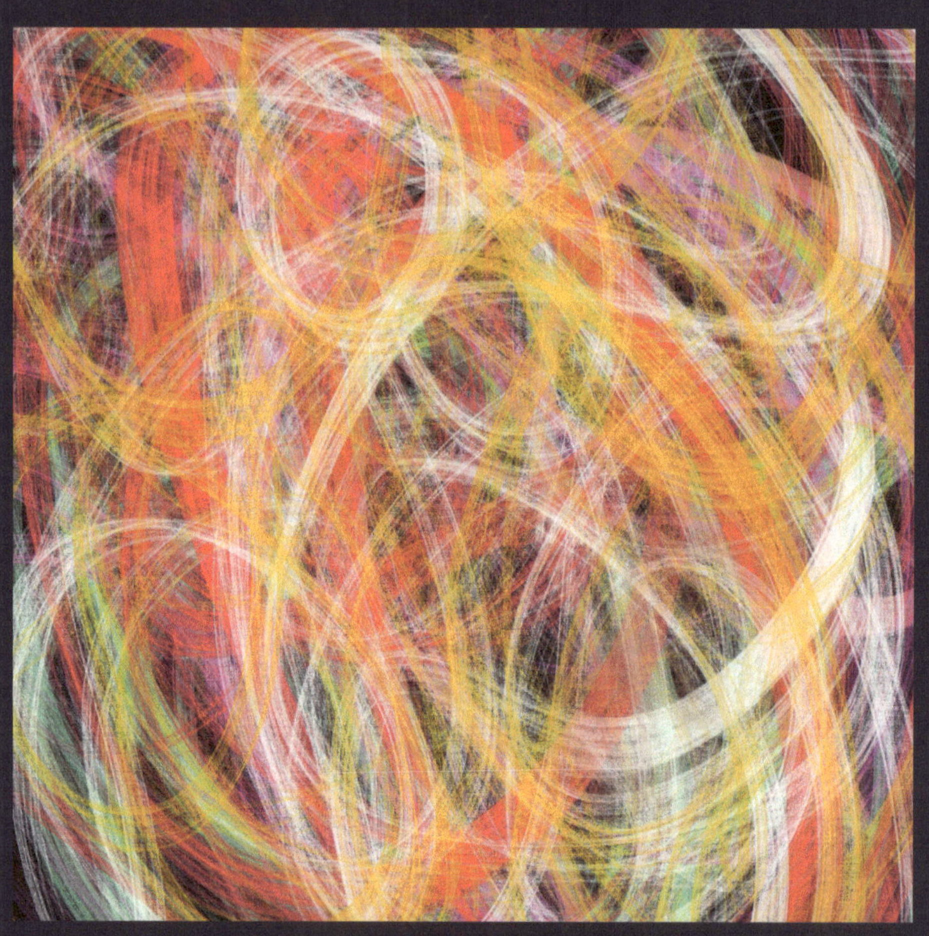

Joseph T.Y. Lee **Labyrinth of Depression**
Oil on Canvas (digital) 4000 x 4000 pixels, Dec 2021

Hayley Mitchell Haugen

> "In depression, the lights are off, but somebody's definitely home.
> She just can't make it to the door to let you in." – Martha Manning

Blue Wife lights the NO VACANCY sign

when she loses her womb to adhesions:
two caesarians, the gallbladder mess,

creating a sticky web of scarring.
And now, there simply is no room

for desire, for mothering, no nourishing space
inside herself to welcome wayward travelers,

her friends. Left behind like two forgotten suitcases,
her ovaries ache sometimes, reminding her

of places she's been, but the blue estrogen pills
hold her just this side of nostalgia,

keep menopause at bay. She is neither
too hot, nor too cold. No anger

no weeping, yet her rhythms are in flux,
despite what the doctors say. Forgetful,

she makes half a bed, eats half a sandwich,
drifts midway through her son's homework

assignment, her mind wandering
some stark hallway, pondering renovations,

like choosing wallpaper. What could emerge
from this blank space? She can't see it.

She's done with decisions,
just done managing it all.

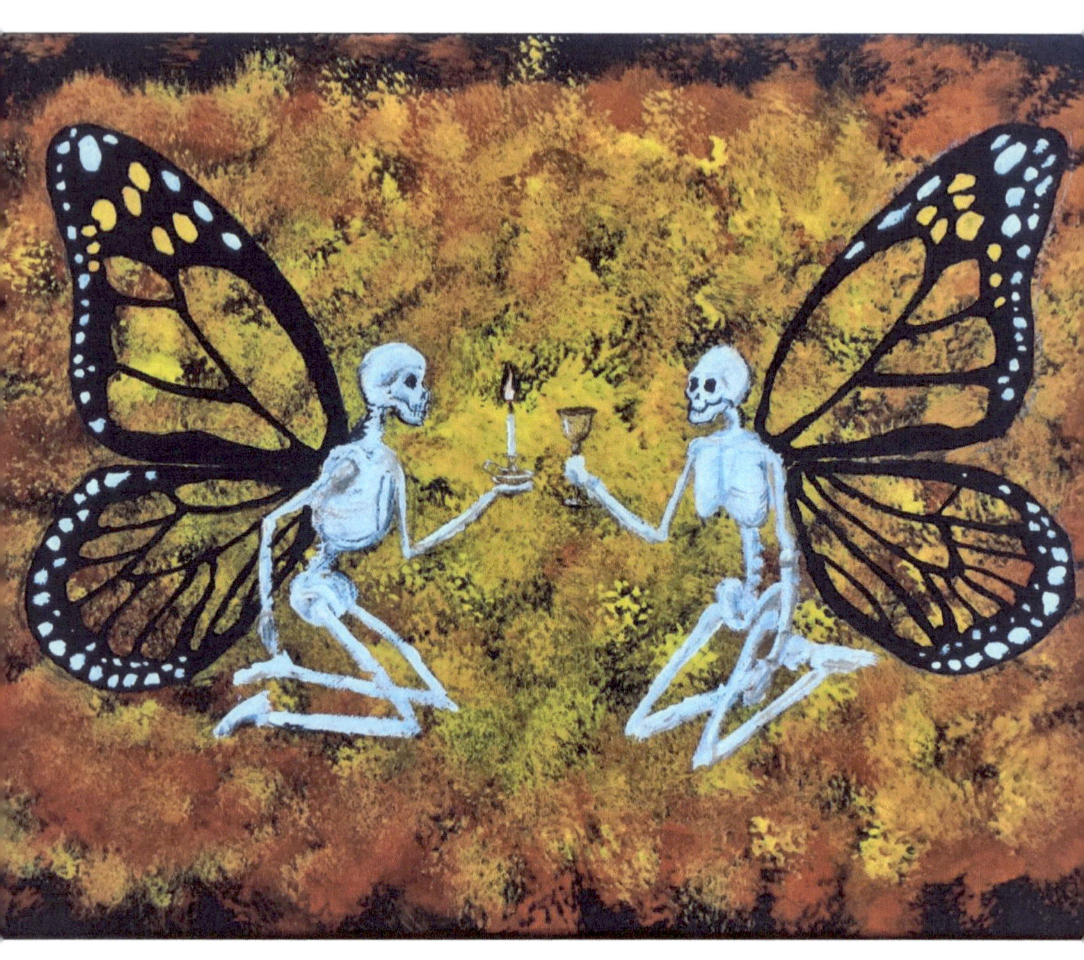

Diego Share Vargas **Shared Breath**

Kimberly Jae

How to Know when to Shoot: A Training Manual

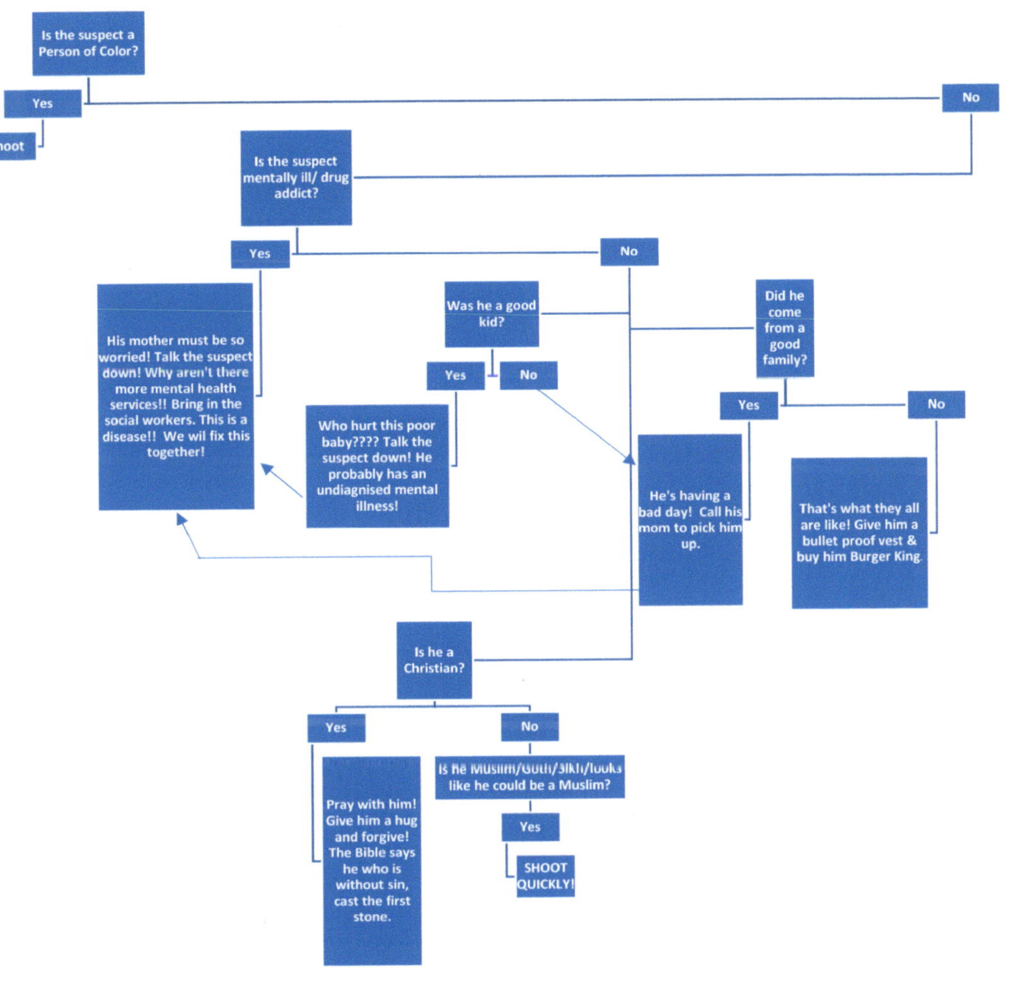

Kimberly Jae

My To-Do List

Body
    ☒**Wake up**   ☒Roll ¾ quarters of the way over   ☒Make sure I'm still alive   ☒Take medicine

Autoimmune System

☒Wake up/ Roll ¾ quarters of the way over/ What is *that*. . .!?!/ **Pump** adrenaline/ Activate **death color coded T-cells**/ Wreck this body/ Rip out the disease/ **I SEE YOU**/ I see the monsters that masquerade as organs/

☒Call in the semi-automatic/ Load the shells/ **This monster**/ This beast in healthy organs' clothing/ Must die/ Must shoot up this space until **the disease** is gone/ **Kill** the organs to save **the body**

☒Take aim/ yank the charging handle back/ smash the release/**trigger happy**/ Recycle the gas **capture** the force/ recoil/ Eject

☒High velocity/deforming/bullet with fragmentation/ **chew up** this body/ eat **the organs**/

e   x   p   a   n   d

/collapse/

devour the clothing/ fill **the whole** with threads and make-believe bandage/ skin elastic/ close around the entrance/ **bloody tears bled**/ sacrifice/ crucify/

☒Why are you crying/ Why aren't you proud me/I got the bad guys/**Look**/ we can be safe now/ I didn't mean to hurt your kidney/ I'm sorry/ **Forgive me**/ Give me praise/ Give me gold stars and hugs/ I just wanted save us from us/**I love you**/ I love **us**/ I didn't mean it/ Why aren't you cheering./ If only you would cheer, then I wouldn't have to hurt you/ Sometimes you just make me so angry/ I only do this because I love you/ Why do you make me hurt you!/ STOP CRYING

☒I AM NOT CRAZY/ WHY ARE <u>YOU TRYING TO EMBARRASS ME</u>/ NO ONE WILL EVER LOVE YOU AS MUCH AS I DO/ I KNOW WHAT IS BEST FOR US!!!!!!!!!!!!!!!!!!!!

☐ ~~KILL US!!!!!!~~

(Is **this** still called living?)

☐Brain matter cease/ stop the battle/ what memories/ what **is normal**/ my body is trying to kill me

<u>Brain</u>

☐Tighten chest/ Tingle into fingertips/ Insides quiver/ **hide** themselves behind the bone/ **I'll be good** this time/ ragged appearance/ **do not know the defense** / Sleep a lot/ **Be** very **still**

☐Wake up/ Roll ¾ quarters of the way over/ Make sure I'm still **alive/ Cry** a little bit/ **Take medicine**

Kimberly Jae
Chunky Black Girl Listens to Lizzo or Ode to Spanx

The stretch marks and I
been together awhile
Someone's lifetime in fact
She leaves these cute little
messages across my body
Finger tipped chiseled codes
People volunteer to translate
I imagine this one is oracle
Tells the blessing knowing me will be Or simply a recipe

Thanksgiving tables and chimney stocking For I give life
Make empty spaces into home
Maybe they tell the secrets of the world Trace history into

Rivers and valleys across millennia
I disavow self-heartbreak
These are not clawed out self-esteem
Waiting for skinny body to worship herself
Nor shredded shards of broken over healed skin Rather, heal over the
circumstance

Admittedly,
I get a kick out of those things I
And not supposed to love
I just refuse to be
One of those things I
am not supposed to love
And these stretch marks
Where God touched me and said, "let there be life" Will forever be life
A love letter to self
Awaiting to be read

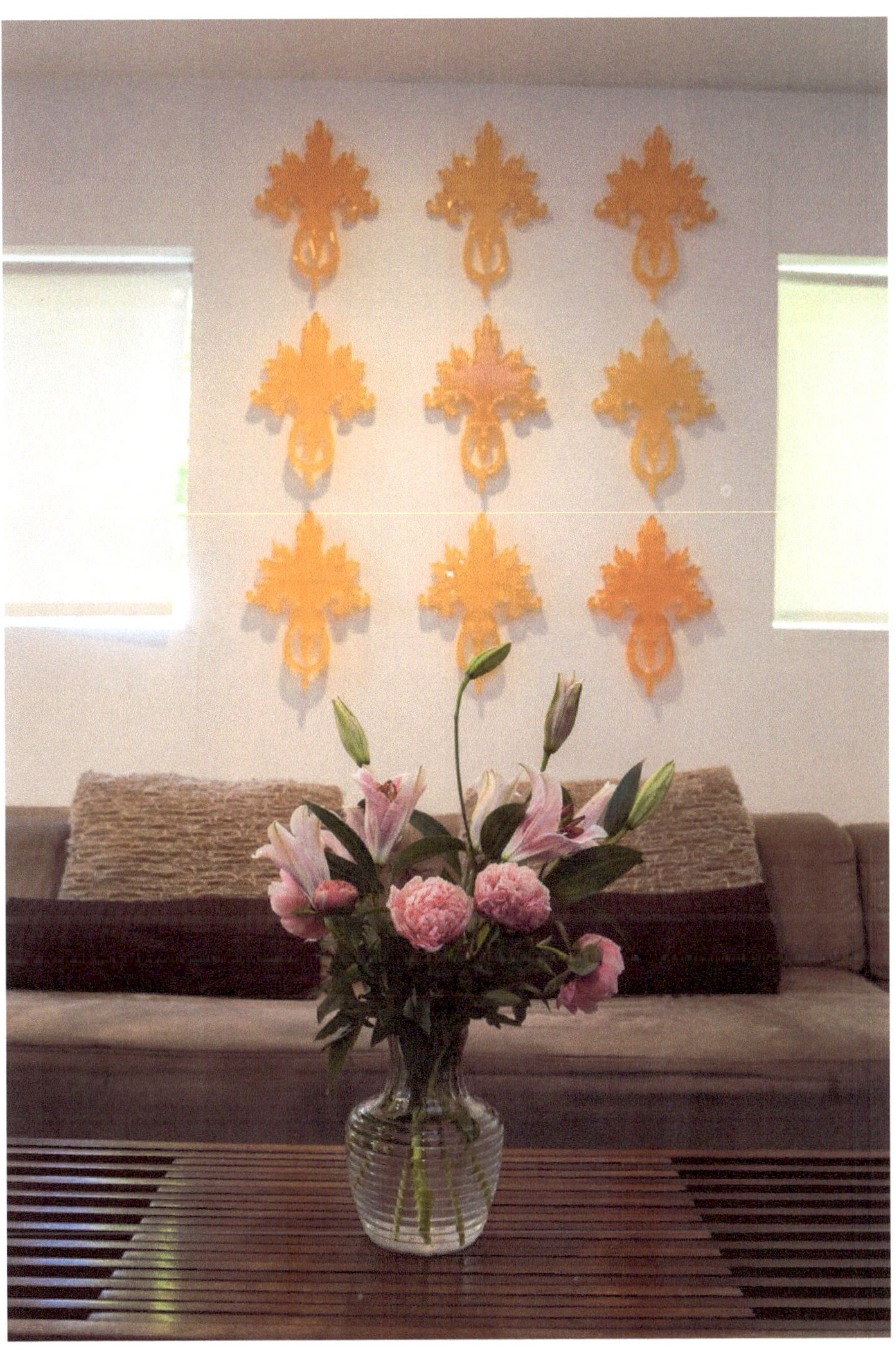

Nik Orlando **Golden Fleur Sculpture: Resin and Pigment**

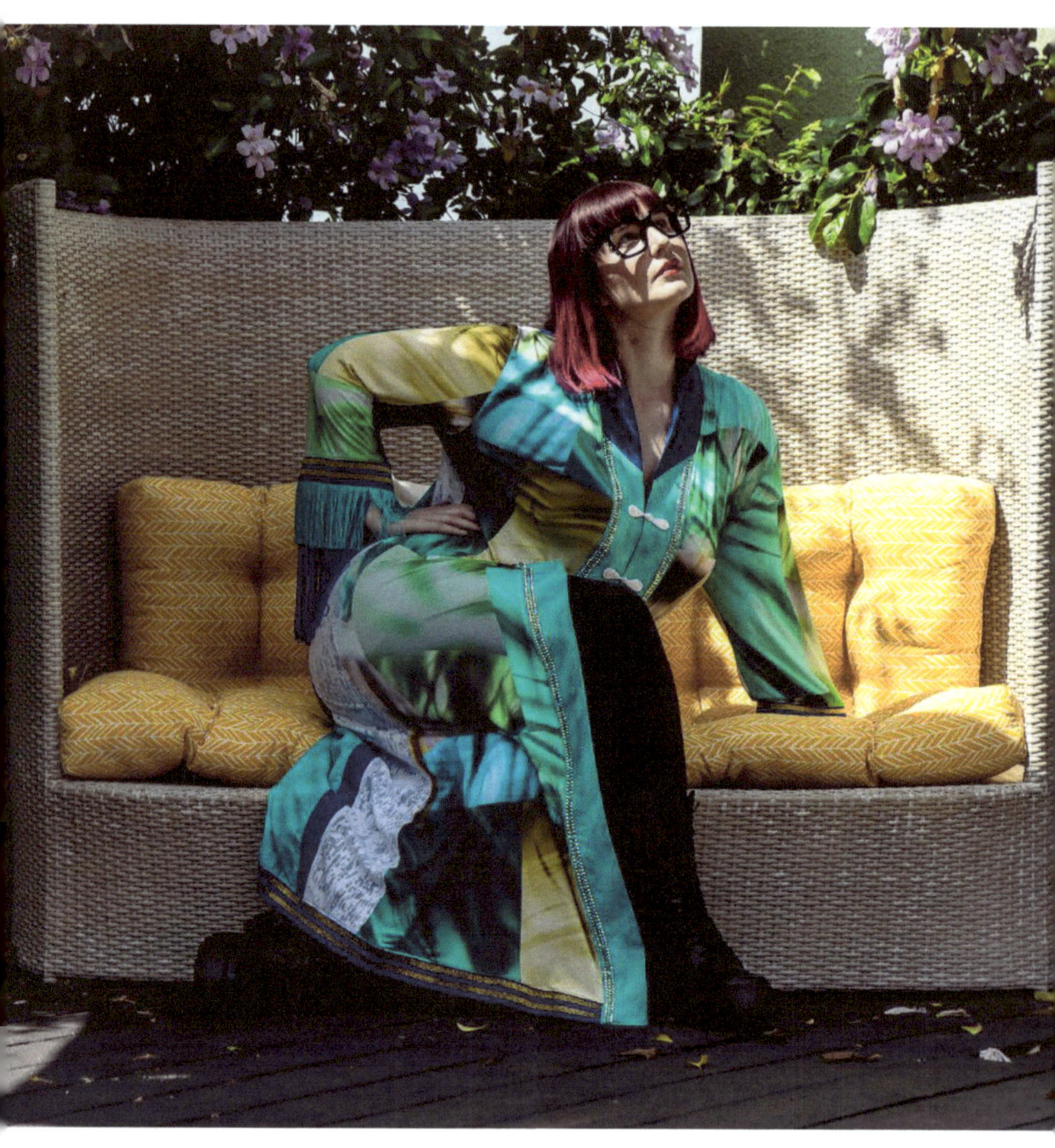

Nik Orlando
**Enter the Dragon Nikomo (Robe / Cover Up):
Cotton, Jersey, Rhinestones**

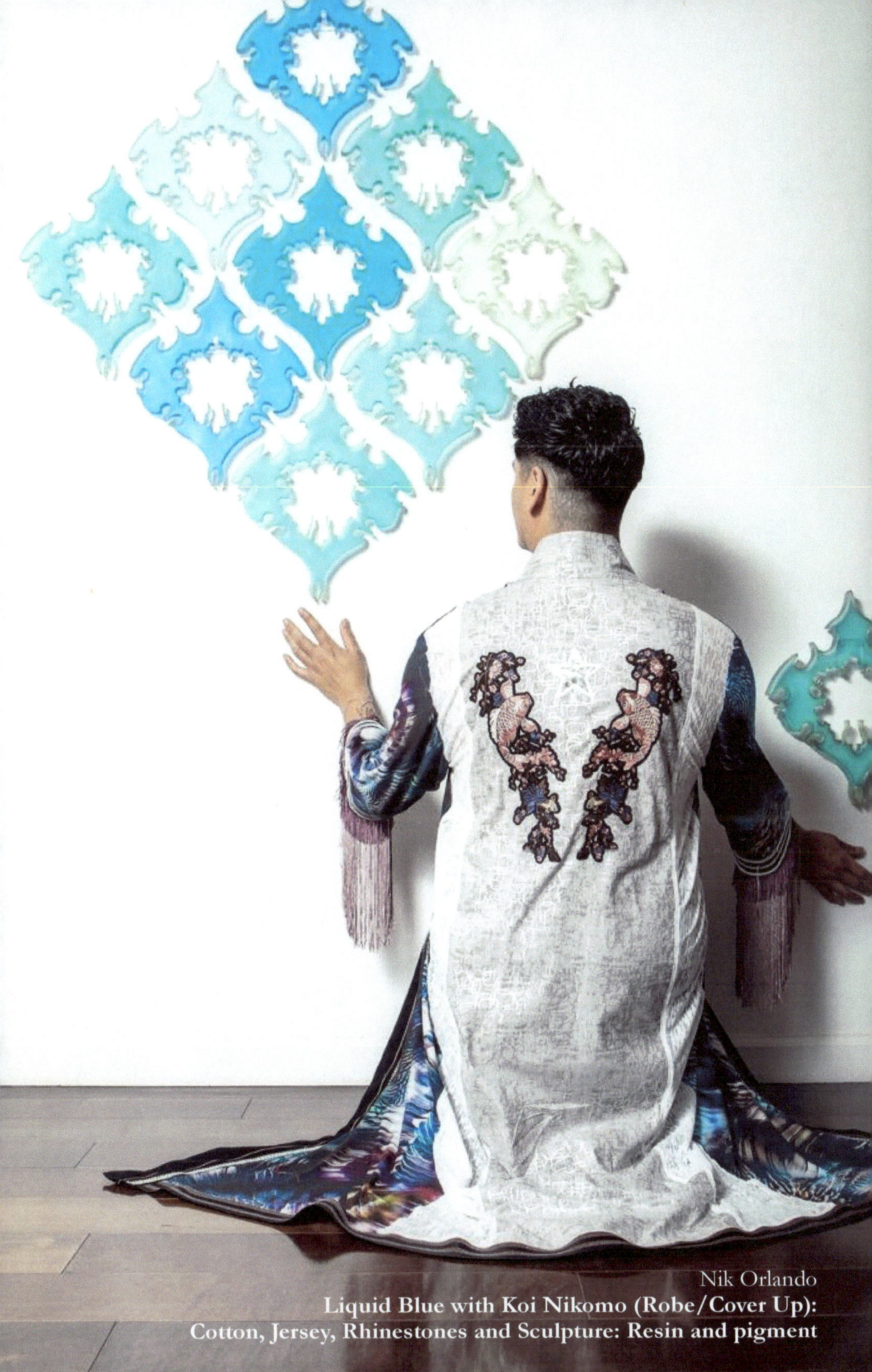

Nik Orlando

Liquid Blue with Koi Nikomo (Robe/Cover Up):
Cotton, Jersey, Rhinestones and Sculpture: Resin and pigment

Brian L. Jacobs
Pilgrim Prayer

step
into this body of peace
an isle of exile addicted to violence
do not relinquish
but assuage me in this fag divination
a pilgrim defined in this cage of a Homocaust pogrom
un blessing me
by the non-gods in this cosmological bag
my poetic vertigo babel
on route to a new communal order of equals
unamalgamated contagions pilgrim'd in each pink step
an invitation
to errant imprints
a privilege in anguish
in an odor
of vagabonds
where strangers congregate on shores of banishment
I perform it queer
kept my charities of perversity vulnerable to my vestment
this Homocaust of mine
die endlosung der judanfrage
to chant
imperviousness saves me
my performance
obscured
and amazes the ripening pods that hang afloat
carrying the seed spit considerable distances
to my expulsion
on this paper tiger's moral geography
intersects
in human and nonhuman ahimsas
at war with consistency in porous boundaries
this terminus register
of cantor articulation song
ruminates
on a history of my persecution
for poetry does not come out looking good an inadequate act following
atrocities
for how to go on living after Homocaust
but in these writings

steps towards clarity
queer queer clarity
skipping with the reaper scribes poesy
and these poetic screams transcend mass extermination
for the purpose of my healing

patch worked rhizomes meditating in phrontistery steps
there is a study of schedules in my torn jeans
and sometimes these steps stumble diversely
in unpredictable realms and question poetry
that task
the savage ritual state
with this narrative not innocent
but a guilty confederacy that should admit itself so
a prerequisite
for denial injurious
this hollowed temple body impious design
evinces nothing sacred or transcendental
but base and plebeian levelling this reject of heroism
as I am an islet in Europe or maybe a cow

and if an oppressor was never a child or heroin a flower incontrovertibly
I have never been loved my body a non-cell
pilgrimaging souls fecundity to my loving scars
when poetics refuses me again and rather than pity me
envision flying peacocks with galloping antelope
and drum charging oxen
lifting the throb at the avalanche pedestal
and in the shadow of the Beats pilgrimaging into India's Samsaras
I can be
a cypress tree
and if writers are whores
I am a rhythmic complication
I am suburbia's Walt Whitman hopeful claiming the world I want to enter
a stranger to myself as a liquescent sift
greased
on counterfeit disposition
not missing the chance to listen to myself
for I am not a clock but intricate hopscotch

and even if this man sits at a blank page
it doesn't mean words suit this cosmogony
with these trippings'steps
poems inhabited by spirits' ash heaps
and colorful victims
more present than the living word
against despondency
and offend libretto's authority
in need of talisman daring captured by my own authority to relish errantry
tenderness yet appears
and I wanted to step into and write Oh L'amour but poetics refused me
reaching for something sane in this poesy never ever fear again
at that moment of errantry in cosmology's crucible
who does this occupied space belong to in forgiveness
narrowly remembering generosity and hospitality
unpurposefully artless as in times of war

and witnesses are ugly whores I teach
that dispute history
and go on about the inadequacies of this world
am I a citadel liberated through the James Baldwin house
those who do not know this peppermint set in platinum

must pray to death and beauty
that glory and eternity can still toil the sower
while the ulcers come aching and obliterated amongst this sacred geography
this pilgrim a consultation with dirt hounded and neglected
in mutants of memory as ash'd heretics
are burned like stick fire on the faggot heaps
marking the unremarkable reified in my recenter
there is no self
without this earth holding me down to do this work
I am an edit before death
burying my brethren burning tongue
into blossom I fall quiet
the drink of nightmares facing east west
creating language illusions
as maps plowing divergent semantic turfs

claiming the world I want to enter
a valediction to understanding that soaks the creeping figs
that resemble vaginas or is it kidneys
and even the freeway has memory under poetry's frowns
so I walk unarmed pageants of me
to mutate in a community minus strangers
as a pilgrim called again to myself creating texture
in my step compassions scars
queering me dust
formed steps against
the uniformed killing industry maps
calling me to myself
to travel magnetic tracks
fraught from the scarecrow immigrant whipped strawberry fields
planted near the orange groves of my suburban youth

and
I step

Brian L. Jacobs
Past Is Plunge

push
some islet

against
the wall

lingering
eye

illume
the depths

the past
is plunge

Brian L. Jacobs
Thatches of Dearth

the pilgrim massif
its homonym

inventors
of the quiver

drunken ascension
unsnarl'd

canna meanders
the inestimable thatches of dearth

Brian L. Jacobs
Lips of Earth

symmetry
of plantings

hinders
me

submitting
to an unfounded order

abutting a catalogue
of fixed forms

affectation
or coquetry

lips
of earth

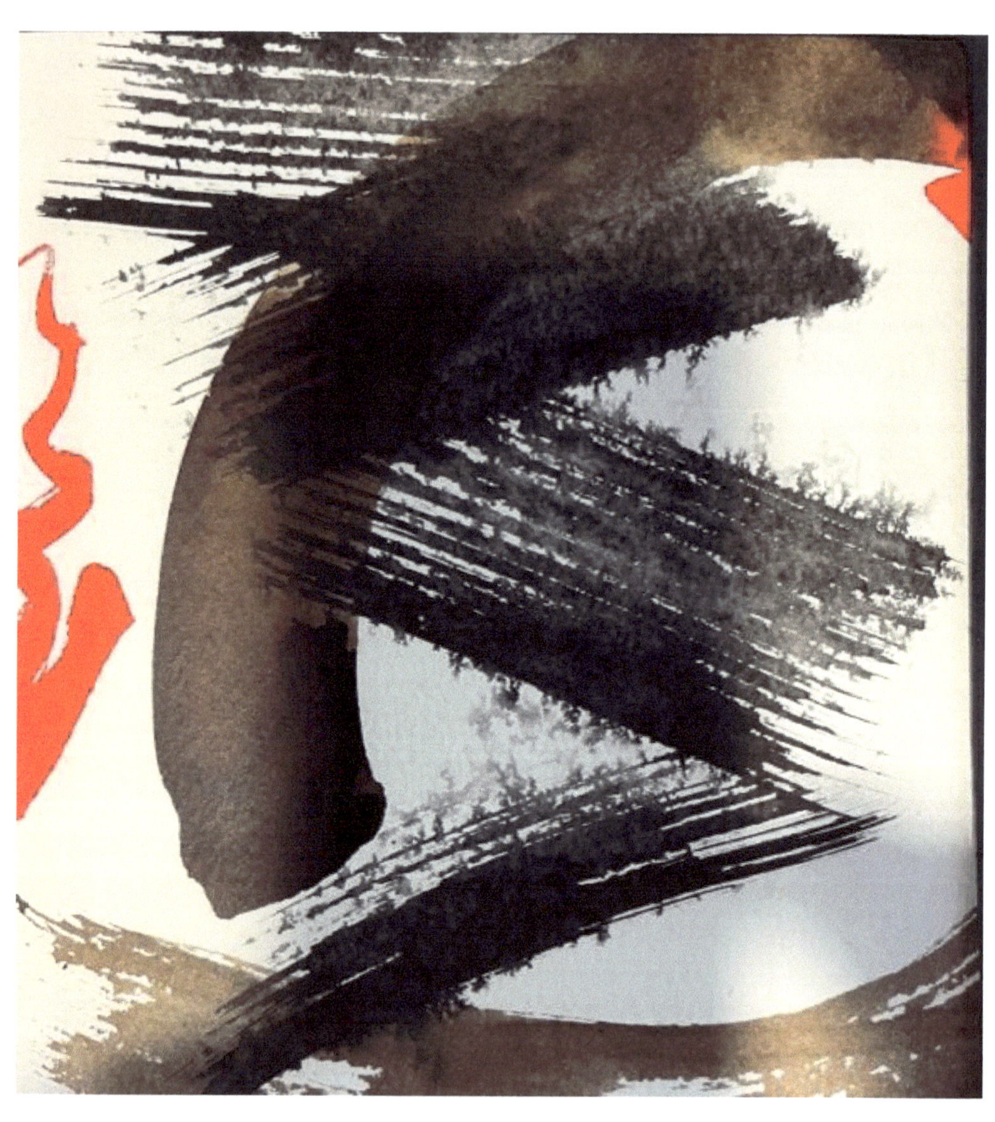

Janet Meskin **Abstract Surprise**

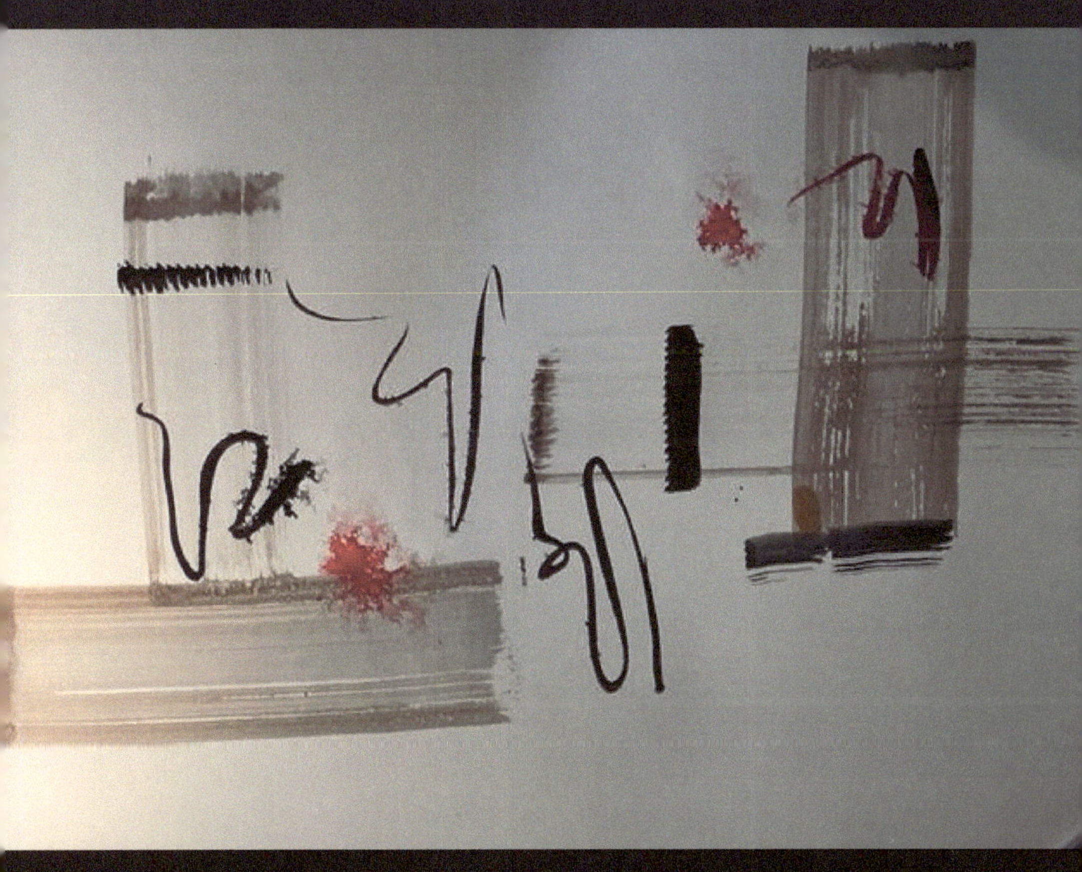

Janet Meskin **Question/Answer**

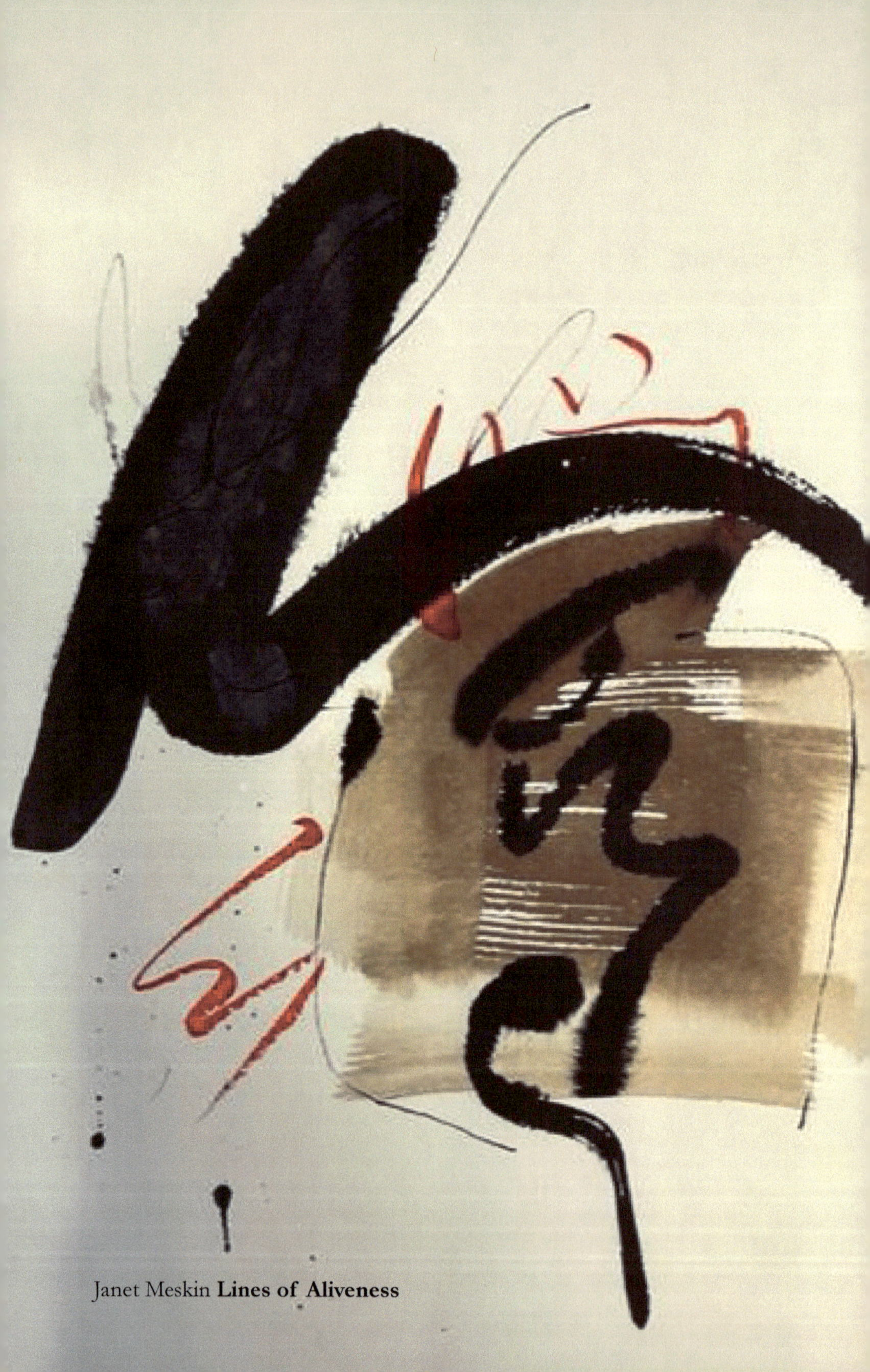

Janet Meskin **Lines of Aliveness**

Ali Telmesani
Lo, in the Month of Dhul Qiddah

Lo, in the month of Dhul Qiddah when tremble the stars and the elements
gleefully, and the cool winds bring bouquets of green pastures all 'round,
see how the birds they surrender their wills to all matters of Soul,
gathering nigh on the banks of the Zagra intent on attainment.
Simurgh, what course are we set to commence when the Hour arrives?
O in the name of the One, the Real through whom creation occurs,
Light of the East and the West, O unique among noblest of Lords,
Sovereign of Days set in stone at the base of the holiest of all trees,
Banyan of banyans long gracing the sanctum sanctorum of eons flown.
Prophets whose footsteps led millions 'pon millions of weary novices
out of the shadows and onto the righteous Path of the wayfaring
courtesans destined to sit at the foot of the Most Compassionate,
destined to feel the soft hem of Her garment of purely Divine Light--
they are the ones who possess the sound knowledge bestowed outright
by the Right Guided, Most Wise, the preeminent Master of all Time.
Even the Paterōn's famous diviners debase themselves utterly
under the weight of Her aegis as surely as dew dangles happily
evening through morn on the delicate branches and leaves, when the heralding
sun rides her chariot forth from beneath the horizon all-conquering.

Song most sublime! Muse of the Real! Give us a sign of your
master's devices lest we be the ones who move blindly in ignorance.
All of Creation depends on the whim of the Merciful's Calamus
sprung from the void of preternal infinity, timeless, beginningless,
out from behind the ethereal veil that divides the dimensional
plains of both subtle and un-subtle beings. Her well-spring is limitless
bound not by spatial nor temporal factors, for She is the source of all
matters both spatial and temporal. Spirits and bodies bend wilfully--
demons unholy and angels of pure composition and parity--
when the command is sent forth from on high, when the Aleph obediently
cries, thus releasing the Letters and Names from their mansions celestial.

Well-spring of well-springs, the oceans would readily dry, and the skies cleave
open before every word that described Your true eminence
ever ran out at the closing of day, at the Hour of Reckoning.
Fluttering hearts ever-fluctuate as You disclose your Self fleetingly,
lightning-like, snatching the Self out of body, transforming alchemically,
lightening, lifting the spirit, de-rusting the mirror reflecting candescently
luminous God and Her rarefied Love, making living the dead, clearing
everyday dust from its surface, allowing the Names of the Merciful
ever to flow and to fill all Creation, to paint her in archetypes
pure and eternal, that we may regard the Compassionate's masterpiece
free of perversion by ego's insidious conquest for dominance.

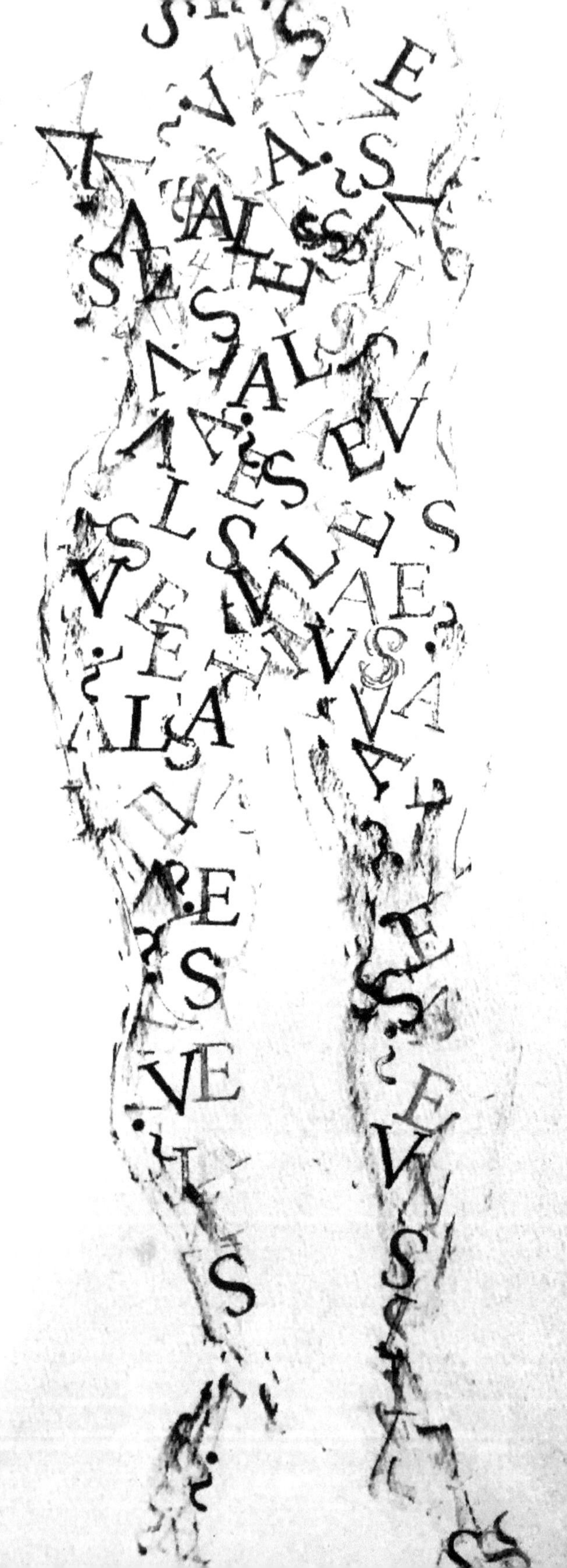

Julie Patton
Untitled

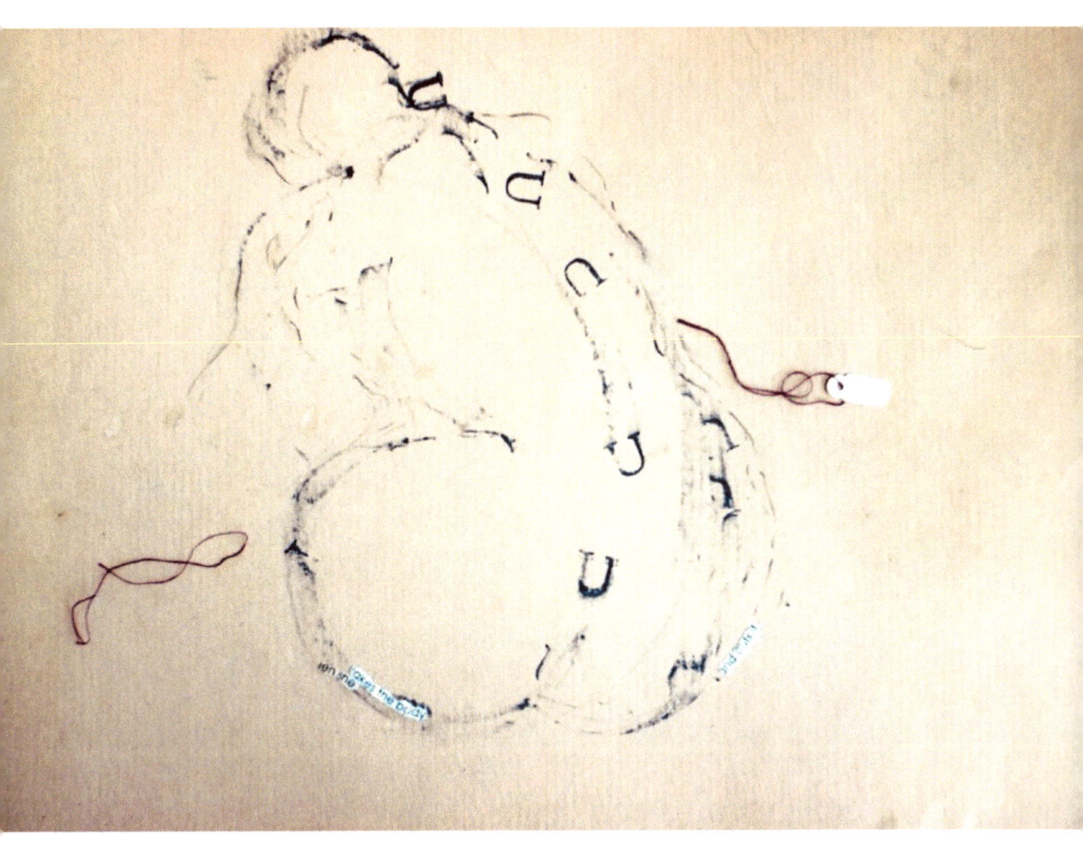

Julie Patton **Untitled**

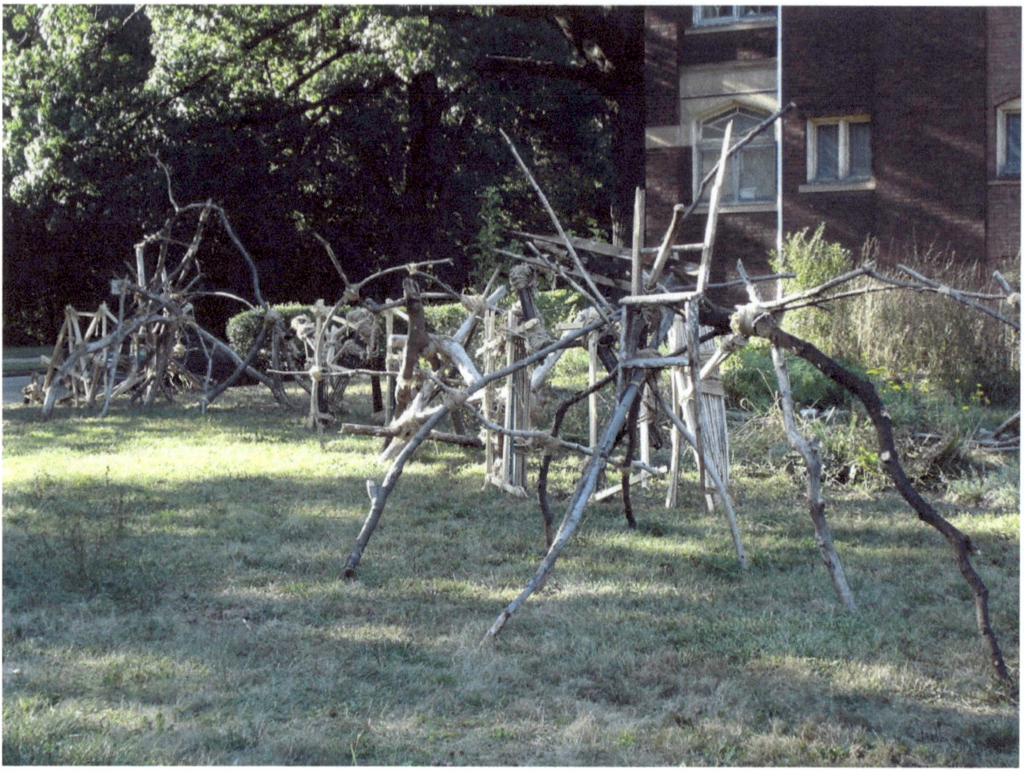

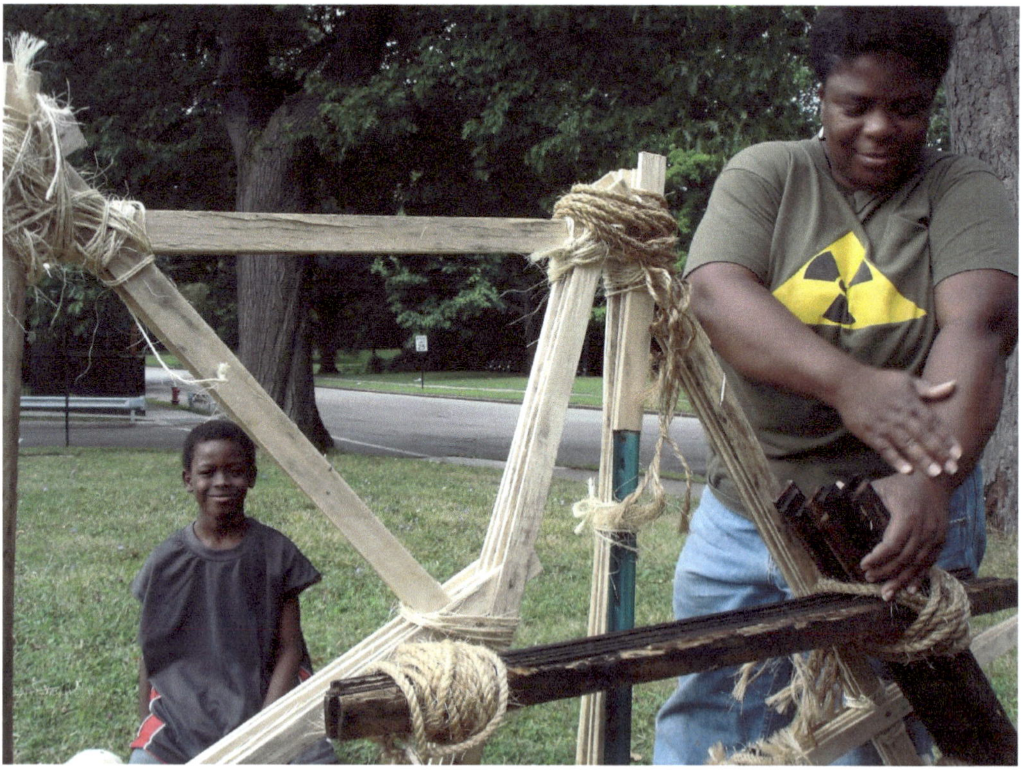

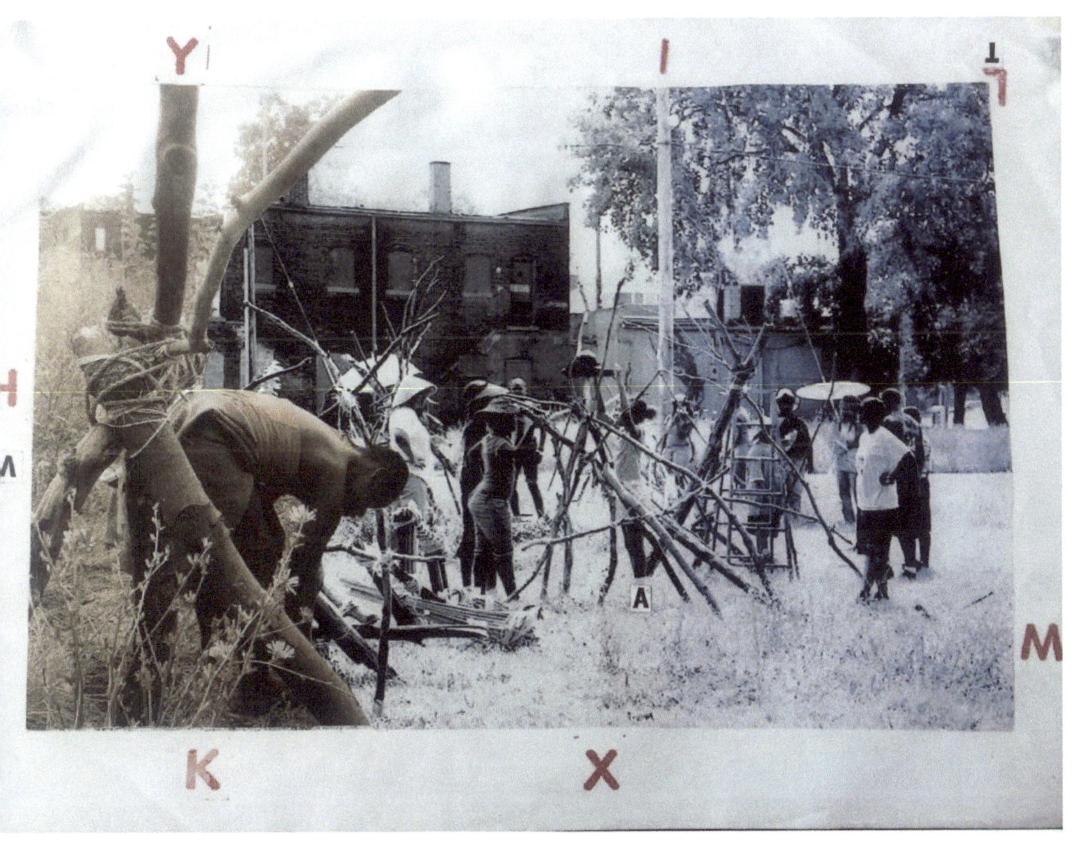

Julie Patton **Alphabet Fence: Everything There Is to Say on Earth**

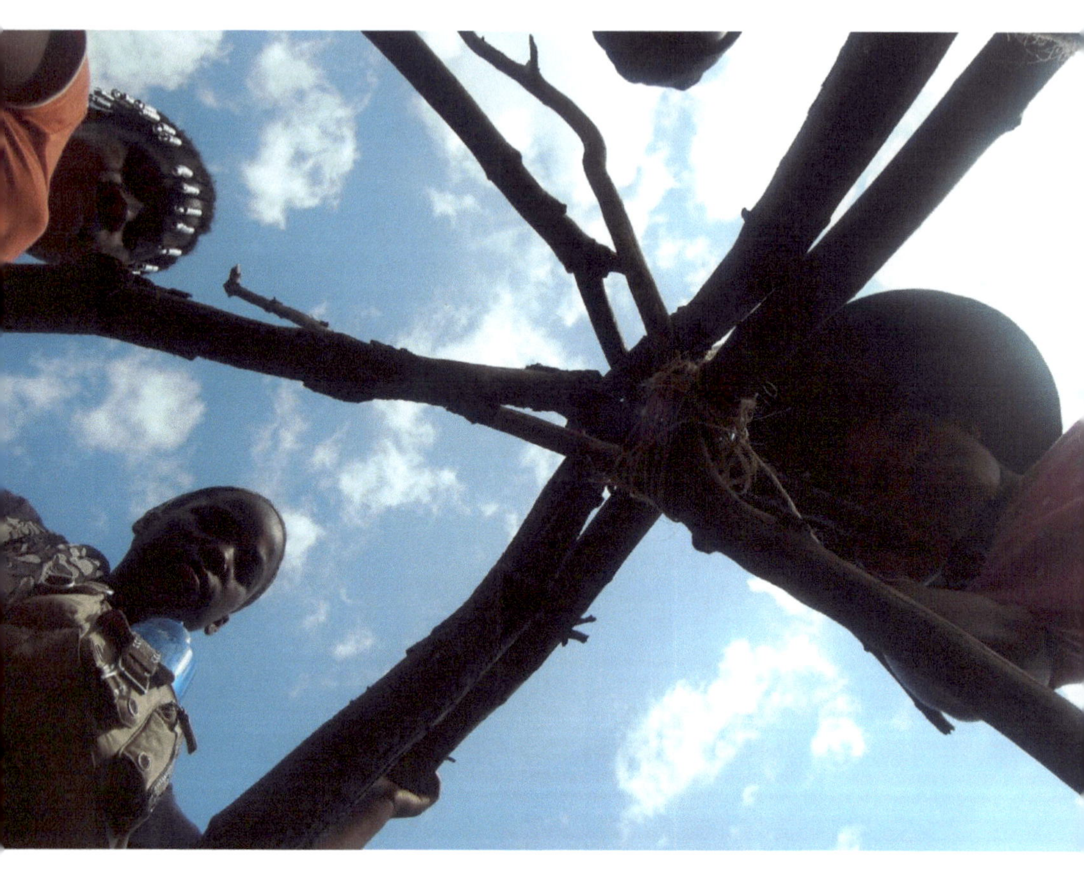

Julie Patton **Alphabet Fence: Everything There Is to Say on Earth**

CONTRIBUTORS

Ignatius Valentine Aloysius earned his MFA in Creative Writing from Northwestern University, where he won the distinguished thesis award for fiction. He teaches as an adjunct lecturer at Northwestern's Weinberg College of Arts and Sciences and in the Writing Program at the School of the Art Institute of Chicago (SAIC). Ignatius is the author of the literary novel *Fishhead. Republic of Want* (Tortoise Books, Chicago), and his writing has appeared in *Tofu Ink Arts Press, Third Coast Review, TriQuarterly, The Rumpus, Newcity, The Extraordinary Project*, among others. He was a 2020-21 Creative Writing Fellow for the Ludington Writers Board and the Ludington Area Center for the Arts in Michigan. Ignatius is co-curator of the popular reading series, Sunday Salon Chicago. He also sits on the curatorial and diversity boards at Ragdale Foundation in Lake Forest, Illinois. @ignatius2u / www.ignatiusaloysius.com

Abol Bahadori has actively shown his work in the UK, Washington DC, Maryland, and Virginia. His first major solo show was in PEPCO Edison Place Gallery in DC with more than 85 paintings on display (2011), later in Aron Gallery, DC (2012) and DESI Gallery Arlington, VA (2013). His works are regularly selected and awarded by the Art League Gallery, Alexandria, VA, with a solo show in 2021. He also routinely been juried in for Washington DC's most anticipated art event; The Washington Project for Arts (WPA) Auction Gala. He has worked in various creative fields throughout his career. As a fabric designer, graphic designer, art director, and currently creative consultant, he's solely relied on fine arts and his continuous painting process as a source of inspiration. As well as a foundation for his professional life, painting is also his livelihood. He considers himself more of a colorist. For Abol color is everything. Color comes before shape and form. It creates space, dimension, and—most importantly—feelings.

Charlie Becker is a retired speech pathologist who now studies and writes poetry with the Community Literature Initiative in Los Angeles. He also has helped bring poetry to under-served high school students through the Living Writers Series and L.A. Unified School District. Charlie's first book of poetry and drawings, Friends My Poems Gave Me, was published by World Stage Press in 2016. He has also had poems published by Passager Journal, Comstock Review, The Dandelion Review, and Silver Pinion. Charlie lives with his partner, Aubry, in Laguna Woods, California.

Gordon Blitz at as a child was called a sissy, girlie, fag, queer, and homo. Getting towel whipped, stomach punched and spit on were part of his world. His father, who died after Gordon's Bar Mitzvah, berated him with shouts of "Walk straight." Gordon never found his writer's voice until he retired in 2017 from forty years of accounting and became a passionate writing machine. During 2020, Gordon had published work in Whoa Nelly Press, Wingless Dreamer, Two Hawks Quarterly, the Santa Monica College Journals Chronicles and On Going Moments, and Gay Wicked Ways. In 2021 his best-selling novel "Shipped Off" was published and is also available as an audiobook. On February 2022, his second novel "Fathers and Other Strangers" was published. Ten of his autobiographical stories are available on the Queer Slam Episode 21, podcast called "Just Gordon." Gordon has been a member of the oldest LGBTQ synagogue in the world Beth Chayim Chadishim since 1990. https://soundcloud.com/queerslam/ His blog URL is: https://culturecritique.blog/

Hayley Mitchell Haugen holds a Ph.D. in 20th Century American Literature from Ohio University and an MFA in poetry from the University of Washington. She is currently Professor of English at Ohio University Southern, where she teaches courses in composition, American literature, and creative writing. Her chapbook *What the Grimm Girl Looks Forward To* appears from Finishing Line Press (2016), and poems have appeared, or are forthcoming, in *Rattle, Slant, Spillway, Chiron Review, Verse Virtual,* and many other journals. *Light & Shadow, Shadow & Light* from Main Street Rag Publishing Company (2018) is her first full-length collection. *The Blue Wife Poems* is forthcoming from Kelsay books in 2022. She edits and publishes *Sheila-Na-Gig online* and Sheila-Na-Gig Editions.

Jones Irwin teaches Philosophy and Education in Dublin, Republic of Ireland. His vision is of a postmodern existentialist, with a dash of noir mixed in with a progressivist ethic. He has been featured before in Tofu Ink.

Brian L. Jacobs is a poet and editor of Tofu Ink Arts Press. Brian grew up in Southern California and has been teaching GATE English and Humanities for thirty one years in both K-12 and college settings. He lives in Pasadena and has been married for 17 years to Thye, a Professor of Nursing and a Nurse Practitioner. Both Thye and Brian are currently PhD candidates and will finish this year. Brian was the assistant to the Poet's Allen Ginsberg and Julie Patton while studying at Naropa. During this time he also on a peace pilgrimage with Buddhist monks commemorating WWII walking through Europe, the Middle East and India. Brian is also a three time Fulbright Scholar, which has allowed him to study in Brazil, where he studied its water issues; China, where he studied its vast 10,000 year history; and Japan, spending time to participate in a case study in one of its small towns near the Japanese Alps. He had also earned a National Endowment of Humanities grant to China, studying its philosophies and histories, a Fund For Teachers grant visiting South Africa, Swaziland and Lesotho, plus earning other various grants that have taken him to places all over in the United States. He also taught teachers at a university in Fuzhou, China for five summers under grants from SABEH. Subsequently he has earned an Earthwatch grant to the rainforest of Ecuador, to study climate change and caterpillars and he recently earned another Earthwatch Senior Fellow Grant to teach teachers in Acadia, Maine studying climate change and crabs. Brian has been to 110 countries and had visited all 50 states, practices Yoga and is a proud vegan. Brian's poetry has been published in several publications including, *Shiela-Na-Gig, the Crank, The South Florida Florida Poetry Journal, Progenitor Art and Literary Journal, GRIFFEL, Foxtail, Rip Rap, The Bangalore Review, Sunspot Lit, Anthropod, Pa'Lante, Dark Moon Lilith Press, Black Tape Press, Genre, Inky Blue/Celery, Red Dancefloor Press, Entelechy, 1844 Pine Street, Pasta Poetics, Trouble and Praxis.*

Queen Kimberly Jae is an award-winning Slam Poet ranking in the top 30 slam poets in the world by PSI in 2018. In 2019, she had a stroke, rendering her disabled. She developed a language-based disability called Aphasia, which affects her ability to speak, read and write. Undaunted, she has since won multiple fellowships, competitions and have been published. Forthcoming publications include *In Between Spaces: An Anthology of Disabled Writers*(November 2022, Stillhouse Press) and *Tupelo Quarterly.*

Cynthia Kerby is a visual artist, former design professor, jewelry designer, curator, and co-founder of True Ideas, a design studio in Evanston, Illinois. Her visual art has been included in ArtPrize, and shown at the Evanston Art Center and Noyes Cultural Arts Center, at Woman Made Gallery in Chicago, at White Bear Center for the Arts in Minnesota and in the Valade Family Gallery at the A. Alfred Taubman Center for Design Education, in Detroit, to name a few. She has curated exhibitions at The Westchester Children's Museum in New York and at Space 900 in Evanston. Cynthia's conceptual Coronavirus mask was included in the Port Townsend Wearable Art Exhibition. She was a featured artist in (Re) An Ideas Journal in New York and also a recipient of a Ragdale Foundation Artist Residency in Lake Forest, Illinois. Cynthia earned her MFA in Visual Communication from The School of the Art Institute of Chicago. As a visual artist she shows familiar objects in unfamiliar ways and makes observations of life's frailties or uncertainties through a lens of personal awareness and curiosity. Her focus is to create work that facilitates change in human behavior and the role she plays in promoting public awareness towards action.

Karin Falcone Krieger writes poetics, stories, essays, reviews and articles which can be seen in *Tupelo Quarterly, The Laurel Review, BlazeVOX and Contingent Magazine*. She taught freshman composition as an adjunct instructor from 1999-2019, and holds an MFA from the Jack Kerouac School of Disembodied Poetics at Naropa University. Her other projects can be seen at karinfalconekrieger.com

Claire Lawrence is a storyteller and visual artist living in British Columbia, Canada. She has been published in Canada, the United States, United Kingdom, Greece and India. Claire's stories have appeared in numerous publications including: *Geist, Litro, Ravensperch, Brilliant Flash Fiction*. She was nominated for the 2016 Pushcart Prize. Her artwork has appeared in Inverted Syntax, A3 Review, Black Lion **Journal**, Esthetic Apostle, and Haunted to name a few. She was nominated for Best of the Net (artwork) 2021-2022. Her goal is to write, create and publish in all genres, and not inhale too much paint.

Joseph T.Y. Lee has more than ten years of experiences in branding, marketing and retail communications. He lives in both Singapore and Malaysia. In 2019, he started his own agency, JLTY Atelier, which specialises in brand and product development. From 2010 to 2013, he volunteered at Project X, a human rights organisation based in Singapore that provides social support and health services to people in the sex industry. A linguistic graduate and polyglot, he speaks English, Mandarin, Malay, French, Cantonese and Hokkien (Chinese dialect). He has passion for the arts and travel, and occasionally, paints & writes poetry.

Amy Lerman, a native Floridian, lives (via the Midwest) with her husband and cats in Arizona and is English Faculty at Mesa Community College. Her poems have appeared in Radar, Rattle, Slippery Elm, Smartish Pace, Euphony, and other publications.

Brendan Lorber is a writer, visual artist, and teacher. He is the author of If this is paradise why are we still driving? (subpress, 2018) and several chapbooks, most recently Unfixed Elegy and Other Poems. He's had work in The American Poetry Review, Brooklyn Rail, Fence, McSweeney's, The Recluse, and elsewhere. Since 1995 he has edited Lungfull! Magazine, currently in hibernation, an annual anthology of contemporary literature that prints the rough draft of contributors' work in addition to the final version in order to reveal the creative process. He's also edited The Poetry Project Newsletter, and curated both the Zinc Bar Reading Series and the Segue Foundation Reading Series. His visual art is in The Museum of Modern Art, The Free

Black Women's Library, Opus 40 Gallery, Artists Space, The Free Library of Philadelphia, The Woodland Pattern Center, The Scottish Poetry Library, and in private collections. He teaches fantasy cartography through Uncommon Goods. He lives in a little observatory in a Brooklyn neighborhood that nobody can quite find on a map.

Mario Loprete; I live in a world that I shape at my liking. I do this through virtual, pictorial, and sculptural movements, transferring my experiences and photographing reality through my mind's filters. I have refined this process through years of research and experimentation. Painting for me is my first love. An important, pure love. Creating a painting, starting from the spasmodic research of a concept with which I want to transmit my message this is the foundation of painting for me. The sculpture is my lover, my artistic betrayal to the painting that voluptuous and sensual lover that inspires different emotions which   strike prohibited chords. This new series of concrete sculptures has been giving me more personal and professional satisfaction recently. How was it born? It was the result of an important investigation of my own work. I was looking for that special something I felt was missing.Looking back at my work over the past ten years, I understood that there was a certain semantic and semiotic logic "spoken" by my images, but the right support to valorize their message was not there. The reinforced cement, the concrete, was created two thousand years ago by the Romans. It tells a millennia-old story, one full of amphitheaters, bridges and roads that have conquered the ancient and modern world. Now, concrete is a synonym of modernity. Everywhere you go, you find a concrete wall: there's the modern man in there. From Sydney to Vancouver, Oslo to Pretoria, this reinforced cement is present, and it is this presence which supports writers and enables them to express themselves. The artistic question was an obvious one for me: if man brought art on the streets in order to make it accessible to everyone, why not bring the urban to galleries and museums? With respect to my painting process, when a painting has completely dried off, I brush it with a particular substance that not only manages to unite every color   and shade, but also gives my artwork the shininess and lucidity of a poster (like the ones we've all had hanging on our walls). For my concrete sculptures, I use my personal clothing. Through my artistic process in which I use plaster, resin and cement, I transform these articles of clothing into artworks to hang. The intended effect is that my DNA and my memory remain inside the concrete, so that the person who looks at these sculptures is transformed into a type of postmodern archeologist, studying my work as urban artefacts. I like to think that those who look at my sculptures created in 2020 will be able to perceive the anguish, the vulnerability, the fear that each of us has felt in front of a planetary problem that was covid 19 ... under a layer of cement there are my clothes with which I lived this nefarious period. Clothes that survived covid 19, very similar to what survived after the 2,000-year-old catastrophic eruption

of Pompeii, capable of recounting man's inability to face the tragedy of broken lives and destroyed economies.
Links to the socials
https://it-it.facebook.com/mario.loprete.5
www.instagram.com/marioloprete/www.linkedin.com/in/mario-loprete-7aa22529

Nik Orlando is an educator and artist. I was born in Las Vegas, moved with my family to the tiny town of Shingle Springs, CA when I was 10, I came to Los Angeles to attend college and the city has been my home for the past 32 years. I am intrigued by all art mediums and fascinated by how they can be manipulated to make a vision come alive. For the past several years I have focused on creating resin sculptures and paintings, wearable art. Sculpture and fashion provide a platform for experimentation and backward planning; thinking with the end in mind. I am intrigued by the concepts of layers, reflections, patterns, and symbols. I am driven by the unexpected combination of these constructs to elicit memories of the past and possibilities of the future. I draw inspiration from music, performance, wallpaper, trees, birds, casinos, and mirrors. Every day is a day to live your look and be unexpectedly inspired by what you see and hear.

Brad O'Sullivan (Brado) is a letterpress printer and mechanic by default. He's a writer, teacher, analog enthusiast and proprietor of Smokeproof Press, a letterpress & design workshop in Boulder, where he employs his Tetris skills at arranging glorious heavy metal machinery. He wears pencils, plays typewriters and guitars, endlessly collects useless items, draws stuff and relishes collaborations with writers, artists, musicians and publishers. Recently became disillusioned with the Oxford comma.

Julie Ezelle Patton is a perma-culturist, poet, performer, artist, and sculptor. Her poetics take the form of scrolls, extended texts, limited edition work, performances, and site-specific installations. Patton's performance work emphasizes improvisation, collaboration, and otherworldly chora-graphs, and bridges literary and musical composition. She has taught at Teachers & Writers Collaborative, Learning Thru Art at the Guggenheim Museum, the Studio In a School Program at New York University, Case Western University, Naropa University, and Schule fur Dichtung in Vienna, Austria.

Ali Telmesani is a Creative Writing PhD Candidate at Swansea University in South Wales, UK. His 2018 publication by Claritas Books, London, is entitled 'House of Abbas: The Legacy of Harun al-Rashid'. Whilst pillaging chariot battles from the Iliad and Aeneid for ideas, Ali developed a burning desire to hear dactylic or 'heroic' hexameter in the original Homeric Greek and Latin, but knew neither. Down and out, he resolved to compose his own hexametic poem in English instead, then deflect blame by placing it in the mouth of a principle character/narrator/perfect fall girl, Aya of Herak, from his doctoral project tentatively entitled 'The Zagra Valley Codices'

R.L. Edmondson Vance is an artist who explores feminism and the self. My work is inspired by pre-history, antiquity, pop culture, nature, and cosmos. My art explores ways to present real figures that both myself and others can see their own bodies represented in.

Diego Share Vargas is a LA based multimedia artist with an undergraduate degree from UCLA who makes their art in their free time when not working as an EMT or Covid Compliance Officer. Their roots come from Oaxaca Mexico and their art explores the complexity and plurality of identity, survival, scx, anticapitalim, and honoring lived experiences. Pre-Pandemic they performed regularly as part of the cast of the Rocky Horror Picture Show at the Nuart Theatre in Santa Monica. Diego links are to zines they have written with art, poetry, and intergenerational knowledge.
The Beauty of Belonging: Biracial Chicanx Narratives
https://www.flipsnack.com/quijoteanonimo/the-beauty-of-belonging.html
Sepulveda Basin: Metal y Tierra
https://www.flipsnack.com/quijoteanonimo/sepulveda-basin-metal-y-tierra.html
Documenting Funds of Knowledge: Medicine and Midwife Family Narrative
https://www.flipsnack.com/quijoteanonimo/documenting-funds-of-knowledge-medicine-and-midwife.html

Brian Yapko is a lawyer whose poems have appeared in Tofu Ink, Prometheus Dreaming, Wingless Dreamer, Gyroscope, Cagibi, Society of Classical Poets, Chained Muse, Abstract Elephant, Poetica and other publications. He lives in Santa Fe, New Mexico.